HOT Chilli Cookbook

**Hot and fiery recipes
from spicy world cuisine**

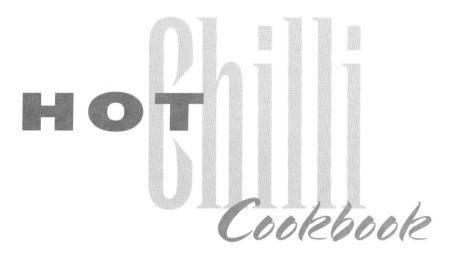

Hot Chilli Cookbook

**Hot and fiery recipes
from spicy world cuisine**

Edited by Jenni Fleetwood

Select Editions
Vancouver

Select Editions

First published in Canada in 1999
by Select Editions
8036 Enterprise Street
Burnaby, BC V5A 1V7
Tel: (604) 415-2444
Fax: (604) 415-3444

ISBN 1-89663-97-6

A QUINTET BOOK
This book was designed and produced by
Quintet Publishing Limited
6 Blundell Street
London N7 9BH

Creative Director: Richard Dewing
Art Director: Clare Reynolds
Designer: John Strange
Project Editor: Clare Hubbard
Editor: Jane Donovan
Illustrator: Shona Cameron

Typeset in Great Britain by
Central Southern Typesetters, Eastbourne
Manufactured in Hong Kong by
Regent Publishing Services Ltd
Printed in China by
Leefung-Asco Printers Ltd.

CONTENTS

INTRODUCTION

PIQUANT, PUNGENT, OR packing a powerful punch, chillies are valued by cooks the world over for the flavour they provide, and although they have been traditionally associated with hot countries, they are becoming increasingly popular in cooler climes, thanks to international travel and improved marketing. Visit a supermarket in Stockholm, Wellington or Washington, and you are likely to find fresh chillies on the vegetable racks, dried chillies and chilli powder with the spices, and hot pepper sauces and salsas alongside other condiments.

Chillies have been cultivated for centuries, ever since the ancestors of today's Mexicans discovered a species of wild capsicum which not only tasted good, but treated their tastebuds to a whole new sensation. From the initial spark, the species evolved rapidly, and today there are more than two hundred different varieties of chilli, ranging in strength from mild to extremely hot.

The Aztecs were very fond of chillies, and it is reputed that the emperor Montezuma had his cooks prepare thirty different dishes every evening, many of them spiked with one or more types of his favourite flavouring.

Early Spanish and Portuguese explorers were seduced by the charms of chillies, and took the brightly coloured flavourings with them when they left the shores of Central and Southern America. Soon chillies were being grown in North and West Africa, in Madagascar and throughout India, where they were seized upon with delight as an alternative to black pepper, which had been the favoured spice up to that time.

Chillies rapidly reached China, where they were to become an important part of Szechuan cuisine, and also spread to Southeast Asia. Thailand, Vietnam and Korea embraced the chilli with enthusiasm, valuing it as much for its appearance as its flavour.

Today chillies are cultivated wherever conditions permit, although the major producers continue to be Mexico, the American states of New Mexico, California, Texas, Arizona and Louisiana, and Thailand. They are very easy to grow, even in cooler regions (although the flavour will be less intense). Even a few plants will reward the grower with a crop of delicious chillies, which can either be used immediately or frozen.

As this collection of recipes proves, chiles can be used in appetizers, soups and main dishes of very type. They make marvellous sauces, relishes and pickles. It is worth getting to know at least a handful of the different varieties, for each has its own distinctive flavour.

Used fresh, chillies add flavour or fire to salads and salsas; grilled and skinned, they have a smoky taste that is so good that they are often served solo, streaked with olive oil; pounded or puréed, they make their presence felt in sauces and stews. In a stir-fry, they can play a starring role, or simply supply a subtle undertone.

Not surprisingly, chillies have a particular affinity for green peppers, and are often grilled alongside these, their less flamboyant cousins. The combination works particularly well in vegetarian dishes, which can often be somewhat bland.

Handle chillies cautiously: they contain capsaicin, an ingredient which can cause irritation to tender skin, and considerable discomfort if it comes into contact with the nose or eyes. Capsaicin is not removed by water, so always wash your hands very thoroughly with soap after handling chillies or – better still – wear gloves. Thin surgical gloves are particularly useful.

If you are wary about chillies, use them sparingly at first, remembering that as a general rule unripe (green) chillies are cooler than ripe red ones, and that most of the fire resides in the membrane and seeds. Experiment with different varieties: Anaheims, for instance, are milder than jalapeños, which in turn generate less heat than habaneros.

Get to know the varieties of dried chilli, too. With a selection of these in your pantry, together with tinned chillies, hot pepper sauces, pastes and powders, you'll have a fine range of flavourings at your fingertips.

A GLOBAL GUIDE TO FRESH AND DRIED CHILLIES

WHEN BUYING FRESH chillies, look for specimens that are firm, shiny, dry and heavy with a fresh clean aroma; avoid those that are discoloured or limp. Rinse and dry, then wrap in absorbent kitchen paper and store in the salad compartment of the refrigerator, where they will keep for 2 to 3 weeks. If chillies are kept in plastic bags, moisture will build up and they will spoil; if not kept in the refrigerator, they will quickly shrivel and become limp.

Remember that the heat is in the membrane or vein as well as the seeds, so when a recipe calls for the chilli to be seeded, the membrane needs to be removed as well. If a hotter flavour is required than the chilli you are using will provide, simply leave the seeds and membrane intact. It is worth noting that everyone's heat tolerance varies, and what one person finds hot, another will not. It is also true to say that tolerance to the heat of chillies can be acquired. The more chillies you eat, the more you will be able to eat with enjoyment. In Mexico it is not unusual to see children eating chillies as if they were cherries.

Once you have become accustomed to chillies, it is well worth experimenting by combining two or three varieties in the same dish, thus imparting a different flavour. The jalapeño is widely available in the United States, but a chilli-lover is likely to scoff at the ordinariness of the jalapeño, favouring a serrano, a habanero or a Thai bird's-eye chilli instead. An amateur may brag about how hot he likes his chillies, but a true connoisseur will talk about the underlying flavours – the earthy, slightly chocolate flavour of the poblano, the hot-sweet intensity of a cayenne, the fiery fruit flavour of a habanero.

DRIED CHILLIES

Like wine, dried chillies have many different flavours, and it takes a connoisseur to detect the subtle differences. They vary from rich smoky and woody flavours to fruity flavours redolent of cherries, plums or damsons, those that have a distinct citrus flavour and even some with a chocolate, aniseed or coffee flavour. It takes time to develop the palate by learning about the different flavours, but it is time well spent. Chillies can transport an ordinary dish to new culinary heights, as their depth and richness of flavour is incomparable.

The drying process intensifies the flavour and gives it a real punch. On drying, the natural sugars concentrate and produce the great depth of flavours that are present.

When buying dried chillies, check that they have no discolouration or spots and are clean, not dirty or dusty. If the chilli is split, much of its oil will have been lost, resulting in an inferior taste. Store in an airtight container for 3 to 4 months, certainly no longer than 6 months.

As with fresh chillies, there are many different varieties of dried chillies and if one is not available, another, or even chilli powder, can be substituted. If powder is used, the flavour will, however, not be as good. Any fresh chilli can be dried, but the more obscure varieties are difficult to find outside their country of origin.

MIX AND MATCH

If a particular type of chilli is specified in a recipe and is unobtainable, either substitute one of the equivalent heat, or use more chiles with a lower heat content.

ANAHEIM — Heat 2–3

The Anaheim, also called the California chilli, is 12 to 17 cm/5 to 7 inches long and 2.5 cm/1 inch wide. The mildest member of the chilli family, it is a cousin of the New Mexico chilli.

The
Anaheim is widely
available fresh, probably second to the jalapeño, and is often tinned and labelled simply 'green chillies'. It is pale green ripening to red, and has fairly thick, smooth skin. Dried, it is a deep burgundy colour, and is one of the most readily available dried chillies. A mild California chilli powder is made from the Anaheim. When Anaheims are used in making dishes like Chilli con Carne, hotter chillies are usually added.

ANCHO — Heat 3–5

The Ancho is actually a dried poblano chilli. It is readily available. Before drying, the chilli is ripened and has a deep reddish-brown, wrinkled skin. Not to be confused with the mulato, which has a blackish tinge to the skin and is neither as sharp nor as fruity as the ancho. About 12 cm/5 inches long, the chilli has a sweet fruit flavour with hints of raisin, coffee and aniseed.

The ancho, mulato and pasilla form the holy trinity of chillies, and are used to make the traditional Mexican mole dishes and sauces.

ARBOL — Heat 8

The *chilli de arbol* is narrow, about 7 cm/3 inches long, and orange-red. It is very hot. It is most often found dried – sometimes labelled only 'dried red chiles' – although other small, hot, dried red chillies such as serranos may also be labelled as *chillies de arbol*. Pure *chilli de arbol* powder may be found in the Mexican section of some very well-stocked grocery stores.

BANANA CHILLI — Heat 2–3

About 15 cm/6 inches long, the banana chilli ranges from pale green to light orange. It has a sweet flavour similar to a green pepper, and thick flesh. The inside of the flesh is often rubbed with chilli powder to impart a stronger flavour. Banana chillies are ideal for stuffing and salads.

CAYENNE — Heat 8

The cayenne is bright red, thin, and pointed, 7 to 17 cm/3 to 7 inches long. It is extremely hot, yet sweet, with a flavour that resembles that of Thai bird's-eye chillies, and is an ingredient in Asian as well as Mexican dishes. It is most familiar dried and ground into cayenne pepper – which will add heat but not much flavour to any dish.

CHIPOTLE — Heat 6

A dried smoked jalapeño, this is dull tan to coffee brown, about 5 to 10 cm/2 to 4 inches long. Often available in tins, these chillies are hot, and are often used with their seeds and membranes intact. The *chipotle grande* is a dried huachinango chilli which is similar in flavour but larger in size.

CONGO — Heat 8

As the name suggests, this chilli comes from the Congo. It is also grown in Mombasa and Zanzibar. A small, green, very hot chilli which turns red on ripening, it is .7 to 1.2 cm/½ inch long.

DE AGUA — Heat 4–5

About 11.25 cm/ 4½ inches in length, tapering to a point, the chilli may be green or red, both colours having a vegetable flavour similar to unripe tomatoes. The red chilli has a slightly sweeter flavour. Grown in South America. Ideal for soups, sauces and stuffing.

DUTCH — Heat 6

Also known as Holland chilli, this bright red chilli is slightly curved, about 10 cm/4 inches in length. It hasa hot sweet flavour and thick flesh. The Thai chilli or red fresno can be substituted. Grown in the Netherlands, it is ideal for soups, casseroles, sauces and pickling.

FRESNO – Heat 6–7

Either green or red, about 5 cm/2 inches in length, the fresno is full and plump, tapering to a round end. It has a thick flesh, and is sweet and hot. Ideal for salsas, stuffing and sauces.

GUAJILLO – Heat 2–4

One of the most common dried chillies available, the guajillo is about 10 to 15 cm/4 to 6 inches in length with a rough burgundy skin. It has a slightly bitter flavour, and the skin is often discarded after rehydration due to its toughness.

HABANERO – Heat 10

One of the two hottest chillies in the world, the habanero – its name means from Havana – is most widely used in the Yucatan, but has gained popularity amongst masochists in the US. The habanero is lantern-shaped and looks like a miniature green pepper, just 5 cm/2 inches high. Its colour ranges from green to orange. When ripe, it is sweet, with a tropical fruit flavour. It is related to the Scotch Bonnet, an equally hot chilli from the Caribbean. Fresh habaneros are showing up in many well-stocked grocery stores, especially those in Caribbean neighbourhoods. Habanero chilli powder and crushed dried habaneros are scarce, but can be found.

HONKA OR HONTAKA – Heat 9

From 3 to 7.5 cm/¾ to 3 inches in length, this orange or red chilli from Japan has a wrinkled appearance.

HUNGARIAN CHERRY PEPPER – Heat 1–3

This round chilli is about 3 cm/1½ inches in diameter. Bright red, it has plump flesh and masses of seeds, is sweet in flavour and mild in heat. Hungarian cherry peppers are grown in Hungary and California. They are ideal for salads.

HUNGARIAN SWEET CHILE – Heat 0–1

About 15 cm/6 inches in length, this sweet chilli is broad at the stem with a rounded end. Bright red, mild in heat with a thick flesh, they taste very like peppers when used as pimientos. Grown in Hungary and California, they are ideal for any dish where heat is not a requirement.

JALAPEÑO – Heat 5–6

The jalapeño, the most widely available fresh chilli in the US, is hot, although there are many varieties of chilli that are hotter. Smooth, glossy jalapeños are usually 5 to 7 cm/2 to 3 inches long, tapering to a rounded end. Although most are sold green, they will turn bright red if left on the bush to ripen. Several raw, chopped and unseeded jalapeños added to chilli will turn up the heat considerably. Roasting jalapeños gives them a marvellous flavour, but they do not need to be roasted. Dried jalapeños are quite scarce. Jalapeño chilli powder is also hard to find. Smoked jalapeños, called *chipotles*, have a wonderful, not at all subtle, smoky flavour. They do

not lose any of their heat in the smoking process. Chipotles are available tinned in adobo sauce. Tart, pickled jalapeños, called *jalapeños en escabeche*, are more often used as a garnish than a main ingredient.

JAMAICAN HOT – Heat 9

These are about 5 cm/2 inches in length, bright red and similar in shape to the Scotch Bonnet or habanero, to which they are related. The flesh is thin, with a sweet, hot flavour. Grown in Jamaica and other Caribbean islands, these hot chiles are ideal for curries, fish stews and chutneys.

KALYANPUR, KESANAKURRU AND KOVILPATT – Heat varies

These are all Indian chillies that are used extensively throughout the country. Green and red.

KASHMIR – Heat 6–8

Closely related to the jalapeño and serrano chillies, they are green or red, about 2 to 5 cm/1 to 2 inches in length. Also called sriracha or siracha. A sauce is made from these chillies in Thailand and sold around the world as an accompaniment to fish.

KENYAN – Heat 2–3

About 2 to 5 cm/1 to 2 inches long, the Kenyan chilli looks like a jalapeño. Often sold when bright green, the chilli turns red when ripe. Grown in Kenya and surrounding countries.

KOREAN – Heat 6–7
Related to the Thai or bird's-eye chilli, this is about 7 to 10 cm/3 to 4 inches in length, thin and slightly curved, tapering to a point. Bright green and thin-fleshed, the chilli has a hot vegetable flavour. Grown in Korea, Japan and California, it is ideal for stir-fries, marinades, chutneys and pickling.

MULATO – Heat 3
About 12.5 cm/5 inches in length, this dried chilli is dark brown. Round at the stem, it tapers to a point. It has a smokier flavour than the ancho, and the predominant taste is aniseed with a hint of tobacco and cherry. Like the ancho, it is sold in Mexico in three different grades, varying in depth of taste and quality.

NEW MEXICO – Heat 3–4
This is the chilli that American Southwesterners rhapsodize about. The New Mexico chilli is a relative of the Anaheim and resembles it in size and shape, but inspires far more passion than its Californian cousin. It is a light to medium green and darkens to a deep red if left on the bush to ripen. These chillies freeze extremely well. They are ideal for salsas, sauces, stuffing and casseroles; the red chillies are also used in red chilli and barbecue sauces.

PASILLA – Heat 4
Also called the *chilli negro*, the pasilla is very dark, purple-black in colour.

It is long and slim like the Anaheim, but has wrinkled skin. The flavour is intense and moderately spicy, with just a bit more heat and none of the sweetness of the poblano. It is more readily available dried than fresh, and is often used in commercial chilli powder blends. The dried poblano is sometimes mislabelled as pasilla. Held up to the light, a dried poblano (called an *ancho*) is reddish, whilst the pasilla is brown-black.

POBLANO – Heat 3
Green or red, this thick-fleshed chilli is 10 to 12.5 cm/4 to 5 inches long. Although only a mildly spicy chilli, the poblano has a complex, earthy flavour with hints of chocolate. Green chilli stews are usually made with poblanos, which can be used in the large quantities required without making the stew scorchingly hot. In a hot chilli, poblanos are used in combination with hotter chillies. The poblano is almost always roasted and peeled. Strips of roasted poblanos, called rajas, make delicious garnishes for chilli.

PRIK CHEE FA – Heat 5–8
A very popular Thai chilli, 'prik' being the Thai name for chilli. A red chilli about 10 cm/4 inches long and fat in shape.

SANTAKA – Heat 9
A very straight, thin deep red chilli, the santaka is grown in Japan.

SCOTCH BONNET – Heat 10
The incendiary Scotch Bonnet is a relative of the habanero, and is often confused with its equally fiery cousin. The Scotch Bonnet is about 2.5 cm/1 inch in length and looks like a tiny tam-o'-shanter in colours of green, yellow, orange and red. Grown in Jamaica and other Caribbean islands, it is not widely available in the US, but a diligent search may find it in a grocery in a West Indian neighbourhood.

SERRANO – Heat 7
Small – about 5 cm/2 inches long – and thin, the serrano is hotter than the jalapeño but not as hot as the cayenne or habanero. The flavour has been described as clean and biting. It is usually sold when glossy green, but it turns red if left on the bush. It can be substituted for the Thai or bird's eye chilli in the ratio of 3 serrano chillies to 1 Thai chilli. Serranos are ideal for guacamole, stir-fries and salsas.

TABASCO – Heat 9
About 2.5 cm/1 inch in length, thin-fleshed with a strong, biting heat. Bright orange or red and used mainly for making the famous Tabasco sauce. Grown in Louisiana and Central and South America.

THAI OR BIRD'S-EYE – Heat 7–8
About 3 cm/1½ inch long, this is a thin, elongated green or red chilli with a pointed end. Thin-fleshed with many seeds, it has a fierce heat. Grown in Thailand, Asia and California, these chillies are ideal for stir-fries and all Asian dishes.

POWDERS, PASTES AND SAUCES

POWDERS

Most dried chillies can be ground successfully, and in parts of the world where the chilli is king, it is not uncommon to see powders made from a specific type of chilli. In the United States, chilli powder is a mixture of spices and herbs. It usually includes pure ground chillies, cumin, oregano and garlic powder, but each manufacturer has an individual blend. Typically ancho or pasilla chilli powder is used. Onion, allspice and salt may also be added. The powder provides an underlying chilli flavour, but not much heat. When it is used for making Chilli con Carne, cayenne or Tabasco sauce, crushed chilli flakes or a pure chilli powder are usually added.

Some spice companies also produce a more fiery blend, called hot or Mexican chilli powder, which will add moderate heat to a dish. Across the Atlantic, chilli powder usually means the pure product: dried chillies that have been coarsely ground. British chili powder is more pungent than the darker American product.

When buying chilli powder, look for a product with a deep rich colour. It should neither be too powdery nor too dry; the best consistency is slightly lumpy, indicating that the natural oils have not been lost. These oils should leave a slight stain on the fingers when rubbed, and the aroma should be intense.

CAYENNE
Made from a single variety of chilli and often referred to as cayenne pepper, this is a pungent, finely ground, deep-coloured spice.

KOREAN CHILI POWDER
Regarded as one of the finest chilli powders in the world, this is a relatively mild, coarse powder which tastes like a cross between paprika and cayenne. It has a glowing carmine colour.

PAPRIKA
Ranging from mild and sweet to warm and pungent – but never hot – paprika is widely used in Hungarian cooking. It has a slightly bitter aftertaste. The colour varies from rose through to deep scarlet. Like all ground spices, paprika is best used as soon as possible after opening. Some cooks recommend storing it in the refrigerator.

RED PEPPER
Made from pungent but not particularly potent chillies, this spice comes from Turkey. The flavour is sometimes enhanced by roasting. Red pepper is also the name sometimes given to cayenne.

CHILLI FLAKES
Also called *chilli caribe*, these are crushed, dried red chillies, usually New Mexico chillies, and are almost always hot. They are often used to give heat to sauces, pickles and sausages.

MAKING YOUR OWN CHILLI POWDER
Preheat the oven to 200°C/400°F/Gas Mark 6. Select one variety of dried chilli or a mixture. Spread out the chillies on an ungreased baking sheet and roast them for a few minutes, until they are somewhat brittle and fragrant. Do not let them darken or they will have an unpleasant burnt flavour. Let the chillies cool, then remove the stems and seeds, cut or crumble them into pieces and place them in a mortar. Grind with a pestle until fine, or use a food processor or spice grinder.

PASTES AND SAUCES

CHILLI PASTE
A thick purée, which varies in intensity, this is sometimes available from specialist delicatessens, either on its own or as an ingredient in a sauce.

SAUCES AND OILS

SAUCES
There are a number of well-known chilli – or hot pepper – sauces, including the famous Tabasco. This is made from the fermented Tabasco chilli, with vinegar and salt. The Tabasco chilli, a cousin of the cayenne, comes from the Mexican state of the same name. It is a small, red, fiery chilli that is not available commercially. Tabasco sauce has been produced since before the Civil War, but as the world's taste for chillies and spicy foods has developed, it has had competition from a great variety of hot pepper sauces.

These include the hot pepper sauces of the West Indies, which are generally based upon the devishly hot habaneros, also known as country peppers or bird peppers (this last because even the birds in the islands have developed a taste for fiery cuisine, and nibble on them). Habaneros rank amongst the hottest peppers in the world. Sauces in the Caribbean give some indication of this: their names include *Jamaica Hellfire, Hell In A Bottle* and *Melinda's XXXtra Hot Sauce*.

OILS
The most familiar chilli oil is a Chinese product, made by heating dried red chillies and vegetable oil together. Many cooks also make their own chilli oil by the simple expedient of steeping dried red chillies in oil. The result not only looks attractive, but creates a flavourful oil for cooking or using in salad dressings. The intensity can be varied by the amount of chillies used, and some cooks add bruised garlic cloves as well.

JERK SEASONING
This is a Caribbean product which originated centuries ago, when the Arawak Indians preserved meat by rubbing strips of it with a mixture of spices and acidic chillies before cooking it slowly over an aromatic wood fire until it was bone dry but still flavourful. The preservation technique was adopted by escaped African slaves in Jamaica to provide food for when they were on the run. Drying of meat in this way was nothing new – native American Indians used the technique and it was also known in Africa – but the jerk spice mixes (so called because the dried meat was known as jerky) became a Caribbean speciality. Soon the technique was extended to the cooking of fresh meat, and steaks and hams were rubbed with a combination of spices and chillies, with additional ingredients, before being chargrilled or smoked. Families

guarded their jerk seasoning recipes jealously. Some added lime juice or vinegar; others sweetened the mixture with sugar or molasses. Jerk seasonings and sauces remain very popular today, and are sold commercially.

OTHER PRODUCTS

Tinned chillies are also available but it is generally preferable to use fresh or dried chillies. Large tinned chillies can be stuffed, and pickled jalapeños (*en escabeche*) are useful.

USING CHILLIES

ROASTING FRESH CHILLIES

STEP 1

Remove freshly roasted chillies from the grill.

STEP 2

Place chillies in a plastic bag to cool.

STEP 3

Peel off the skins.

REMOVING THE SEEDS

If a recipe recommends seeding a chilli, cut off the stem end, split the pod open and scrape out the seeds and membrane with a teaspoon. Rinse and gently pat dry with absorbent kitchen paper.

ROASTING FRESH CHILLIES

Roasting fresh chillies gives them a wonderful flavour and takes the edge off their heat. It also allows easy removal of the tough skin on some larger chillies, such as Anaheims and poblanos. Smaller chillies, including habaneros, serranos and jalapeños, do not need to have their thin skins removed, but may be roasted for improved flavour.

Place the chillies – whole or in two or three large pieces – in a preheated grill. Cook for a few minutes, turning frequently, until the skin blisters and blackens. Take care, however, not to burn the flesh. You can also grip each chilli in turn with tongs and hold it over a gas flame to blister, or dip it quickly into hot oil. Once the chillies have blistered, place them in a bowl and cover with several pieces of absorbent kitchen paper, or put them in a plastic bag. Leave them to cool, then peel off the skins or rub them off under cold running water, if necessary. Remove the membranes and seeds if you like.

DRYING CHILLIES

Mature fresh chillies can easily be dried. Simply thread them on heavy cotton thread. Use a needle with a large eye and pierce each chilli just below the stem. Hang the chillies in a warm, dry place for about a week. A whole dried chilli, added to a casserole, will give just a hint of heat, and can be removed at the end of cooking. Dried chillies can also be ground.

DRY-ROASTING DRIED CHILLIES

The flavour of large, dried chillies will be improved if they are dry-roasted before being used. Heat a non-stick frying pan, add the chillies and sear them for 2 to 3 minutes, or until they begin to soften and grow plump. On no account allow them to burn, or the flavour will be ruined.

RE-HYDRATING DRIED CHILLIES

To re-hydrate dried chillies, remove the stems and seeds and cut each chilli into two or three pieces. Put them in a deep, narrow heat-proof bowl. Pour in very hot (but not boiling) water to cover. Stir, make sure all the pieces are immersed in water, then let stand for 30 minutes. Pour the chillies and their soaking water into a blender or food processor. Process until smooth, then sieve. Use the sieved sauce in cooking. The chillies can also be simmered in water, beer or stock before being puréed.

GARNISHING WITH CHILLIES

Brightly coloured chillies make a wonderful garnish. Tie a bunch of them with raffia or coloured twine to garnish a large platter of food that features them, or carve one or two into chilli flowers. To do this, choose perfect chillies with smooth, unmarked skins. Rinse each chilli lightly and pat dry with absorbent kitchen paper. Holding a chilli by the stem, slit it in half lengthwise. Scrape out the seeds. Keeping the stem intact, cut the chilli lengthwise into strips or petals. Put the chilli in a bowl of iced water and repeat the process with the remaining chillies. Leave for 10 minutes, until the chilli petals have curled to form flowers. Drain the chillies, dry lightly and use as a decorative garnish.

Chopped or sliced chillies also make a good garnish, as do pickled jalapeños. Simply scatter them over the finished dish to add colour and extra piquancy.

SAFETY FIRST

It is essential to handle chillies carefully: the unwise cook who carelessly rubs his or her eye after chopping chillies is in for considerable pain. The culprit is capsaicin, the oily substance which gives chillies their fiery nature. Capsaicin does not dissolve in water, so it is important to soap your hands thoroughly after working with chillies.

Wearing latex gloves is the ideal answer, but this will not prevent capsaicin from getting onto knives, chopping boards and other utensils. Wash these thoroughly, preferably in the dishwasher.

If you do have the misfortune to touch delicate skin after handling chillies, rubbing the stinging spot with a little shortening may help. Burning lips, tongue or throat can be eased by a swallow of milk, soured cream or yoghurt. Avoid drinking water, which will not help and may even make the problem worse.

DIPS AND SNACKS

GUACAMOLE

Serves 4

The cool appearance of this delicious dip is deceptive: contrasting with the creamy avocado is the fiery flavour of chilli.
Guacamole is great for parties. Serve it with carrot and celery sticks and traditional taco chips.

INGREDIENTS

2 ripe avocados

100 g/4 oz peeled, seeded and finely chopped ripe tomatoes

1 bunch spring onions, trimmed and finely chopped

2 serrano chillies, seeded and finely chopped

1 or 2 jalapeño chillies, seeded and finely chopped

2 tbsp lime juice

1½ tbsp freshly chopped coriander

salt and pepper

shredded lime peel, for the garnish

taco chips and crudités, to serve

Peel the avocados and discard the seeds. Mash the flesh with a potato masher or fork.

Add the finely chopped tomato and spring onions with the chillies and mix together well. Stir in the lime juice with the coriander and seasoning to taste. Spoon into a bowl and flake the top.

Sprinkle with lime peel just before serving with the taco chips and crudités. Guacamole is best eaten immediately, but if it has to be kept, place one of the avocado seeds in the middle, cover and chill for no longer than 1 hour.

THAI HORS D'OEUVRES

Serves 6 to 8

This colourful selection of ingredients on a leaf-strewn platter is a tempting invitation for guests to make their own flavourful lettuce parcels.

INGREDIENTS

30 g/1 oz unsweetened dessicated coconut, roasted at 180°C/350°F/Gas Mark 4 until light brown

3 tbsp finely diced shallots

3 tbsp finely diced lime

3 tbsp diced root ginger or crystallized ginger

3 tbsp chopped dried baby prawns

3 tbsp unsalted roasted peanuts

2 tsp chopped fresh small green Thai chillies

vine or other edible leaves, for decorating platter

lettuce leaves, for serving

SAUCE

2 tbsp unsweetened coconut

½ tbsp prawn paste

1½ tsp sliced root ginger

½ tsp sliced shallot

3 tbsp chopped unsalted peanuts

2 tbsp chopped dried baby prawns

225 g/8 oz demerara or soft brown sugar

600 ml/1 pt water

First make the sauce: roast the dessicated coconut with the prawn paste, root ginger and shallot in a 180°C/350°F/Gas Mark 4 oven for 5 minutes until fragrant, then let cool. Place the peanuts and prawns in a blender or food processor and chop finely, or pound with a mortar and pestle.

Pour the mixture into a heavy pan. Add the sugar and water. Mix well and bring to a boil, then lower the heat and simmer until the sauce is reduced to about ½ pint. Remove from the heat and let cool.

To serve, pour the sauce into a serving bowl and arrange all the ingredients in separate piles on a platter or in small bowls. Have the lettuce leaves ready in a separate bowl. To eat, take a lettuce leaf, place a small amount of each of the garnishes in the middle, top with a spoonful of sauce and fold up into a little package.

CHILLI CON QUESO

Serves 8 to 12

Chilli con Queso is a sort of Southwestern fondue – melted cheese with chillies, onions, garlic and tomatoes. It is a terrific dip for chips, crackers or crudités, or can be a main dish fondue, served with chunks of bread. It can be kept warm by setting the pot over a candle or on a warming tray. For a mild dip, remove the seeds and veins from the jalapeños.

INGREDIENTS

2 tbsp butter

2 or 3 jalapeño chillies, minced

1 garlic clove, minced

1 medium tomato, seeded and chopped

3 green onions, minced

225 g/8 oz grated red Cheddar cheese

225 g/8 oz grated Monterey Jack cheese or white Cheddar

Preheat the oven to 180°C/ 350°F/Gas Mark 4. Heat the butter in a frying pan and sauté the chillies, garlic, tomatoes and green onions for 5 minutes. Continue cooking, if needed, until the liquids have evaporated.

Stir the vegetables into the grated cheese in an oven-proof serving dish. Bake until the cheese is bubbling, about 12 minutes. Serve immediately whilst piping hot.

BEAN DIP WITH CHILLI

Serves 6 to 8

INGREDIENTS

3 or 4 jalapeño chillies

2 tsp corn or olive oil

250 g/10 oz drained and rinsed tinned red kidney beans

250 g/10 oz drained and rinsed tinned cannellini beans

1 or 2 garlic cloves, minced

60 to 75 ml/2½ fl oz tomato juice

1 ripe mango, peeled and sliced

1 tbsp freshly chopped oregano

extra freshly chopped oregano, for the garnish

crudités, for serving

Pre-heat the grill to high. Place the chillies in a grill pan and drizzle with the oil. Grill for 4 to 5 minutes, or until the skins have blistered and blackened.

Put the chillies into a plastic bag and leave to sweat for 10 minutes; then discard the skin and seeds if a milder dip is required. Put into a food processor with the remaining ingredients and blend to form a thick dipping consistency.

Pour into a serving dish, cover and chill for 30 minutes to allow the flavours to develop. Sprinkle with chopped oregano, and serve with the crudités.

▶ *Chilli con Queso*

SPICED AUBERGINE PURÉE

Serves 6

Baked aubergine, puréed with chillies and spices, makes a marvellous, creamy dip. Cumin seeds add crunch.

INGREDIENTS

2 large aubergines, about 450 g/1 lb

4 red Anaheim chillies

4 garlic cloves

grated zest and juice of 1 large lemon

1 tsp ground cumin

1 tsp ground coriander seed

1 tsp ground cinnamon

175 g/6 oz cream cheese

cumin seeds for the garnish

pitta breads and crudités, for serving

Preheat the oven to 200°C/ 400°F/Gas Mark 6. Rinse the aubergine and prick each of them a few times. Place directly on a shelf in the oven and bake for 40 minutes, or until the aubergines are very soft and have begun to collapse. Put the chillies and garlic on a baking sheet and place on another shelf. Cook the chillies and garlic for about 10 minutes, or until the skins have begun to wrinkle. Remove from the oven and put into a plastic bag for 10 minutes. Peel and discard the seeds from the chillies and the skins from the garlic, and set aside.

Let the aubergines cool, then strip off the skin and put the flesh into a food processor with the chillies, garlic, lemon peel and juice. Add the spices. Process to a smooth purée, then add the cream cheese and process again. Transfer to a serving bowl and flake the top.

Chill for at least 30 minutes. Garnish with cumin seeds and serve with pitta breads and crudités.

HOT AND SMOKY FISH PÂTÉ

Serves 6 to 8

You can use any smoked fish for this tangy pâté. Serve with an assortment of crackers. The pâté also tastes good spooned onto celery sticks or as a topping for slices of toast.

INGREDIENTS

450 g/1 lb smoked marlin

50 g/2 oz sweet pickle relish

57.5 g prepared horseradish sauce

1 small onion, chopped

1 celery stalk, finely chopped

1 mild red chilli, seeded and chopped

½ tsp lime juice

1 tsp hot pepper sauce

75 g/2½ oz mayonnaise

salt and pepper

Chop the fish coarsely and place it in a mixing bowl. Add the relish, horseradish, onion, celery, chilli and lime juice, and mix well. Add half the hot pepper sauce and half the mayonnaise. Mix well and taste. Add more hot sauce, according to your taste. Stir in more mayonnaise and mix until the desired texture and flavour is achieved.

CHALUPAS

Serves 4

Tortillas form the basis of many Mexican dishes such as enchiladas, burritos and empanadas. They are often filled with a variety of savoury mixtures, and almost always served with a side dish of refried beans.

INGREDIENTS

TORTILLAS

290 g/10 oz all-purpose flour

1 tsp salt

1 tsp baking powder

1 tbsp lard or shortening

200 ml/⅓ pint water

SAUCE

2 tsp sunflower oil

1 small onion, chopped

2 red jalapeño chillies, seeded and chopped

400 g/14-oz tin crushed tomatoes

FILLING

½ small Webbs lettuce, shredded

200 g/7 oz Refried Beans (page 26)

57.5 g/2 oz grated hard cheese, such as Cheddar

4 spring onions, trimmed and chopped

2 red jalapeño chillies, seeded and chopped

soured cream and lime wedges, for serving

Make the tortillas by mixing the flour, salt and baking powder in a bowl, cutting in the lard or shortening, and adding enough of the water to make a stiff dough. Divide the dough into eight pieces and shape into small balls.

Use a tortilla press, if you have one, to make eight tortillas. Alternatively, place each ball of dough in turn between two plastic bags and roll out to a thin round, 15 cm/6 in across.

Heat a heavy non-stick frying pan and cook each tortilla for about 2 minutes on each side, or until the edges begin to lift and the surfaces are lightly browned. Wrap the cooked tortillas in absorbent kitchen paper and aluminium foil so that they stay hot while you cook the chilli sauce.

Heat the oil in a small pan and gently sauté the onion and chillies for 5 minutes. Stir in the crushed tomatoes and bring to the boil. Reduce the heat and simmer for 15 minutes. Let cool slightly, then sieve to form a smooth purée. Cover and keep warm.

Warm the tortillas if necessary by placing in a non-stick frying pan for about 30 seconds. Dampen the edges, then shape and pinch up the sides of each to form a boat shape.

Fill the tortillas with the shredded lettuce and place the refried beans on top. Spoon a little of the prepared sauce over. Divide the cheese among the tortillas and sprinkle over the spring onions and chopped chillies. Serve with soured cream and lime wedges.

COOK'S TIP

The best way to reheat tortillas is over a direct flame. Pat them with damp hands if they are uncomfortably dry. Alternatively, wrap them in a clean tea towel or serviette and reheat them in the microwave on High for 40 to 50 seconds, or wrap aluminium foil around the cloth package and reheat them in a low oven. If you use bought tortillas, or taco shells, re-heat them as directed on the package.

QUESADILLAS WITH REFRIED BEANS

Serves 4

Quesadillas usually consist of tortillas filled with cheese, folded in half and cooked until the cheese melts. In this snack version, the tortillas are simply sandwiched together with melted cheese, cut in quarters and served with the ever-popular refried beans.

INGREDIENTS

8 freshly cooked wheat tortillas (page 24)

225 g/8 oz grated hard cheese

sliced red chillies, dill pickles, 1 lime slice and 1 stuffed green olive, for the garnish

REFRIED BEANS

400 g/14 oz pinto or black beans, picked over and soaked overnight

3 onions, chopped

5 or 10 garlic cloves, chopped

2 serrano chiles, sliced

300 g/10 oz bacon, diced

salt

3 tbsp vegetable oil

½ tsp ground cumin

½ tsp mild chilli powder

COOK'S TIP
Refried beans are traditionally cooked in a generous amount of lard. This version is lower in fat. To save time you could use tinned refried beans.

Make the refried beans. Drain the beans, place them in a large saucepan, and add water to cover. Bring to the boil and cook for 1 minute, then remove from the heat and let stand, covered, for 1 hour.

Add half the onions to the beans, with the garlic, chillies and bacon. Pour over water to cover and bring to the boil again. Reduce the heat and simmer for 1½ to 2 hours, until the beans are softened. Drain off any excess liquid, then mash or purée the bean mixture to a chunky consistency. Add salt to taste.

Heat the oil in a large frying pan and sauté the remaining onion until soft. Sprinkle in the cumin and chilli powder, cook for 1 minute, then ladle in a scoop of the bean mixture. Cook over medium high heat until thick and darkened in colour, then add another scoop of beans. Repeat until all the beans have simmered to a thick, flavourful mixture. Check the seasoning and add more salt if needed.

Sprinkle the cheese over half the soft, freshly cooked tortillas, and place the remaining tortillas on top. Heat the tortilla 'sandwiches' in a heavy non-stick frying pan until the cheese has melted, then cut them in quarters and serve with the refried beans. Garnish with chillies, dill pickles, lime slices and olive.

SPICY PEPPER PIZZA

Serves 4

Chillies and mixed peppers make for a colourful pizza topping with plenty of flavour. Add sliced pepperoni if you like.

INGREDIENTS

1 tbsp sunflower oil
1 onion chopped
2 garlic cloves, crushed
5 red jalapeño chillies, seeded and thinly sliced
400 g/14-oz tin crushed tomatoes
2 tbsp tomato purée
2 tbsp freshly chopped oregano
2 tsp ground cumin
2 prepared 20 cm pizza bases
2 red peppers, skinned and seeded
2 green peppers, skinned and seeded
2 yellow peppers, skinned and seeded
175 g/6 oz grated mozzarella cheese
50 g/1½ oz stoned black olives

Preheat oven to 200°C/400°F/Gas Mark 6. Lightly oil two baking sheets.

Heat the oil in a pan and sauté the onion, garlic and chillies for 5 minutes. Add the crushed tomatoes, tomato purée, oregano and cumin, and bring to the boil. Reduce the heat and simmer for 10 to 15 minutes, or until the mixture forms a thick sauce.

Spread the sauce over the pizza bases. Slice the peppers and arrange on top of the sauce. Cover with the cheese and arrange the olives on top. Bake for 25 minutes, or until the cheese is golden and bubbly.

VEGETARIAN ENCHILADAS

Serves 4

Tortillas are delicious with a spicy vegetable filling. Vary the vegetables to suit the season. If you keep a pack of ready-to-use wheat tortillas in the pantry, this makes a quick and easy snack.

INGREDIENTS

2 tbsp sunflower oil

1 large onion, thinly sliced

2 garlic cloves, crushed

4 green de agua chillies, seeded and sliced

225 g/9 oz peeled, seeded and chopped ripe tomatoes

1 tbsp tomato purée mixed with 1 tbsp water

2 courgettes, trimmed and cut into matchsticks

175 g/7 oz grated hard cheese, such as Cheddar

6 spring onions, trimmed and chopped

8 freshly cooked wheat tortillas (page 24)

fresh herbs, for the garnish

Chilli Pepper Relish (below) to serve

Pre-heat the oven to 200°C/400°F/Gas Mark 6. Heat the oil in a frying pan and gently sauté the onion, garlic and chillies for 5 minutes. Add the tomatoes and the tomato purée mixture and bring to the boil. Cover the pan, reduce the heat and simmer for 15 minutes.

Stir in the courgettes, 100g/4 oz of the cheese and the spring onions.

Divide the filling among the tortillas and fold them. Place in a shallow baking dish and sprinkle with the remaining cheese. Bake for 15 minutes, or until the cheese is golden and bubbly. Garnish with herbs and serve immediately whilst hot with the Chilli Pepper Relish.

CHILLI PEPPER RELISH

Makes about 125 g/4 oz

This can also be served as an appetizer with crudités and taco chips.

INGREDIENTS

150 g/6 oz peeled, seeded and chopped ripe tomatoes

2 shallots, finely chopped

2 or 3 red serrano chillies, seeded and chopped

1 garlic clove, crushed

1 tsp salt

3 tbsp freshly chopped coriander

1 tbsp lime juice or cider vinegar

7.5 cm piece cucumber, peeled and finely chopped

1 tbsp pumpkin seeds, roasted and then finely ground

coriander sprigs, for the garnish

Put the tomatoes into a bowl and stir in the shallots, chillies, garlic, salt, coriander and lime juice or vinegar. Mix together well, then cover and leave for at least 30 minutes to let the flavours develop.

Stir in the cucumber and pumpkin seeds. Garnish with the coriander sprigs.

▶ *Vegetarian Enchiladas*

EMPANADAS

Serves 4

Empanadas are little pies that may contain sweet or savoury ingredients. As so often, you can use both your imagination and leftovers to the full; this is a basic savoury empanada.

INGREDIENTS

2 tbsp olive oil

1 medium onion, finely chopped

1 small red or green pepper, seeded and chopped

2 medium tomatoes, skinned, seeded and chopped

225 g/8 oz minced beef

1 dried red chilli (arbol or similar)

½ tsp cumin seed

1 tbsp sultanas

salt and pepper

450 g/1 lb prepared pastry dough

Preheat the oven to 190°C/375°F/Gas Mark 5. Heat the oil in a frying pan and sauté the onion, pepper and tomatoes until soft. Add the minced beef and fry until the meat is brown and crumbly.

Crumble in the dried chilli. Use the cumin seeds whole, or for better flavour, crush them using a pestle and mortar. Add the cumin and sultanas to the mixture in the frying pan. Season to taste, and cook for another 10 minutes or so. Let cool.

Roll the dough into eight 12.5 cm/5 in rounds. Divide the filling amongst them, placing it on one half of the round and fold over to seal. Overfilling will make cooking difficult!

Place on a baking sheet and bake for about 35 minutes, until the empanadas are golden brown. Serve hot. Some people prefer to deep-fry their empanadas.

SPICY POTATO PATTIES

Serves 4

Hot chillies and cool mint gives these potato patties a superb flavour.

INGREDIENTS

2 large potatoes (about 425 g/14 oz) diced

1 tbsp freshly chopped mint

1 tbsp lemon juice

½ tsp salt

1 small onion, finely chopped

2 tsp coriander seeds, crushed

1 tsp cumin seeds

¼ tsp chilli powder

2 green chillies, finely chopped

3 tbsp freshly chopped coriander

1 egg

salt and pepper

2 tsp oil

Cook the potatoes in boiling, salted water until they are tender.

Meanwhile, mix the lemon juice, mint and a pinch of salt with the onion in a bowl. Set this mixture for filling the patties to one side.

Drain the potatoes and mash them lightly so that the mixture is still slightly lumpy. Add the coriander and cumin seeds, with the chilli powder, green chillies, coriander and salt. Mix well.

Divide the potato mixture into eight equal portions. Dampen your hands a little and roll each portion in turn between your palms to make a ball. Make a dent in the ball, fill it with a tiny amount of the mint and onion filling, cover the filling and flatten each ball gently to form a burger shape.

Just before frying these patties, whisk the egg and season it lightly. Heat a large, non-stick frying pan and grease it with half the oil. When the pan is fairly hot, dip a potato patty into the egg and put it in the pan. Add

three more patties in the same way. Let them sizzle for a minute or so, then turn them over and cook the other side until they are crisp and golden brown. Cook the remaining patties in the same way.

COOK'S TIP
The patties freeze well, ready for thawing and re-heating when needed. They go well with home made tomato sauce or any of the chilli sauces on page 174.

VEGETABLE SAMOSAS

Serves 4

INGREDIENTS

75 g/3 oz finely diced potatoes

1 tbsp corn or sunflower oil

1 onion, finely chopped

1 garlic clove, crushed

2 red Anaheim chillies, seeded and finely chopped

1 bird's eye (Thai) chilli, seeded and very finely chopped

1 tsp ground cumin

1 tsp ground coriander

200 g/7 oz shelled peas, thawed if frozen

1 red pepper, seeded and diced

1 tbsp apricot or fruit chutney

1 tbsp freshly chopped coriander

4 sheets filo pastry dough

vegetable oil for deep-frying

chilli flowers and fresh coriander for the garnish

Cook the diced potatoes in boiling salted water for 5 to 8 minutes, or until just tender. Drain and set aside.

Heat the oil in a frying pan and gently sauté the onion, garlic and chillies for 3 minutes. Add the spices and sauté for 3 minutes more.

Remove from the heat and stir in the potatoes, peas, red pepper, chutney and coriander. Mix well.

Cut the filo pastry sheets in half lengthwise to make 8 strips, each 25 × 10 cm/10 × 4 in. Place 1½ tbsp of the filling at one end of each strip and fold over diagonally to form a triangle. Continue folding along the strip, sealing the edges with water.

Heat the oil to 170°C/325°F/Gas Mark 3 and fry the samosas in batches for about 5 minutes, or until golden. Drain on absorbent kitchen paper. Serve hot or cold, garnished with chilli flowers and sprigs of coriander.

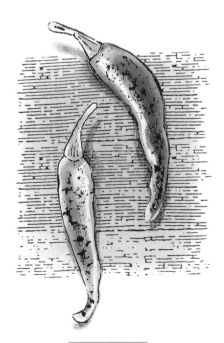

FRIED CORNBREAD WITH BACON AND JALAPEÑOS

Serves 8

This traditional cornbread is flavoured with jalapeño chillies. It is baked in a sizzling hot frying pan, and seasoned with bits of fried bacon.

INGREDIENTS

4 bacon strips
190 g/8 oz cornmeal
75 g/6 oz all-purpose flour
1½ tsp salt
1 tbsp baking powder
2 tbsp sugar
225 ml/8 fl oz milk
150 ml/¼ pint melted butter, or butter and bacon fat
2 eggs, lightly beaten
4 jalapeño chillies, seeded and minced

Preheat the oven to 220°C/ 425°F/Gas Mark 7. Fry the bacon until crisp in a heavy, 22.5 to 25-cm/9 to 10 inch cast-iron frying pan. Lift out the bacon and drain it on absorbent kitchen paper. When the bacon is cool enough to handle, crumble it. Leave about 1 tablespoon of bacon fat in the frying pan. Discard the rest, or combine it with melted butter to make ¼ pint fat for the bread mix. Combine the dry ingredients in a mixing bowl.

Brush the bacon fat around frying pan so it is completely oiled. Put the frying pan in the oven to heat.

Combine the milk and melted butter, then add to the eggs. Stir in the chillies. Pour the liquid into the dry ingredients and stir by hand until the batter is well mixed. Stir in the crumbled bacon.

The frying pan should be hot and the bacon fat just short of smoking. Pour the batter into the frying pan. It will sizzle as it hits the fat. Return the frying pan to the oven and bake the cornbread for 35 to 40 minutes, until it is golden brown. Let cool slightly, then cut into wedges. Serve warm.

FRIED FISH STRIPS WITH CHILLI DIPPING SAUCE

Serves 3 to 4

Strips of fish, coated in egg and flour, then shallow fried, make a tasty snack, especially when served with a chilli sauce for dipping.

INGREDIENTS

57.5 g/20 oz/1¼ lb white fish fillets such as cod or plaice

1 plump garlic clove, halved lengthwise

all-purpose flour, seasoned with salt and pepper, for coating

1 to 2 eggs, beaten

oil for frying

DIPPING SAUCE

4 tbsp soy sauce

2 tsp sesame oil

1 tbsp rice vinegar

½ red or green chilli, seeded and minced

2 tsp toasted sesame seeds

pinch of sugar

½ to 1 small garlic clove, finely chopped

Rub the fish fillets with the cut side of the garlic halves, then thinly slice the fish diagonally. Have the seasoned flour and beaten egg ready in separate shallow bowls. Make the dipping sauce by mixing all the ingredients in a small bowl.

Coat the fish in seasoned flour, then dip in beaten egg, letting the excess egg drain off. Heat a little oil in a frying pan. Add the fish strips, in batches if necessary so they are not crowded, and fry for about 5 minutes, depending on thickness. Drain on absorbent kitchen paper, then serve hot with the dipping sauce.

DEEP-FRIED PRAWNS WITH SPICY TOMATO SALSA

Serves 4

Crisp on the outside, beautifully tender within, large prawns in batter are irresistible.

INGREDIENTS

75 g/3 oz all-purpose flour

2 tsp black sesame seeds

salt and pepper

1 egg, beaten

1 to 2 tsp sesame oil

150–200 ml/¼–⅓ pint water

12 to 16 large raw prawns,
in their shells

vegetable oil for deep frying

SPICY TOMATO SALSA

3 garlic cloves, chopped

2 serrano chillies, chopped

½ onion, chopped

450 g/1 lb flavourful tomatoes,
chopped

2 tbsp freshly chopped parsley

2 tbsp freshly chopped coriander

salt and ground cumin, to taste

juice of 1 lime

Make the salsa by mixing all the ingredients in a bowl. Cover and set aside for at least 30 minutes to develop the flavours.

Mix the flour and sesame seeds. Stir in the egg and sesame oil, then add enough of the water to make a light coating batter. Set aside.

Remove the heads and fine legs from the prawns, leaving the tails intact. With a fine knife-point, slit along the back of each prawn and remove the dark thread.

Heat the oil in a deep-fat fryer to 180°C/350°F/Gas Mark 4. Stir the batter, then dip the prawns into it, allowing the excess batter to drain off. Deep fry the prawns in batches for about 3 to 4 minutes until crisp. Drain on absorbent kitchen paper. Keep hot while frying the remaining prawns. Serve hot with the salsa.

SOUPS

COCONUT AND GINGER SOUP

Serves 4 to 6

This creamy soup originated in Thailand. Use galangal instead of ginger, if you can find it, as it has a milder flavour and is more fragrant.

INGREDIENTS

600 ml/1 pint thin coconut milk

1 shallot, finely sliced

2.5 cm piece root ginger, peeled and thinly sliced

2 lemongrass stalks, cut into 2 cm pieces

6 small whole red fresh chillies

3 kaffir lime leaves, torn into small pieces

1 tsp salt

300 g/11 oz skinless boneless chicken breasts, cut across into 6-cm slices

150 g/6 oz wiped and sliced mushrooms, oyster variety if available

2 tbsp lime or lemon juice

½ tsp Thai fish sauce

3 tbsp freshly chopped coriander leaves, with stems cut into 2 cm pieces

hot cooked rice, for serving

Pour the coconut milk into a saucepan and bring to the boil. Add the shallot, ginger, lemongrass, chillies, lime leaves and salt.

When the liquid returns to the boil, add the chicken and bring to the boil again, then add the mushrooms. Bring back to the boil and cook for 2 minutes or until the chicken is fully cooked. Remove from the heat and stir in the lime or lemon juice, fish sauce and coriander leaves and stems.

Serve over hot cooked rice in bowls. Garnish with extra small red chillies, if you like.

COLD AVOCADO SOUP

Serves 4 to 6

Cold and creamy, with very good colour, this is an excellent choice for summer.

INGREDIENTS

1 or 2 green Anaheim chillies

1 tbsp oil

3 large ripe avocados

180 ml/6.5 fl oz chicken or vegetable stock

275 ml/½ pint single cream

180 ml/6.5 fl oz milk

1 to 2 tbsp lime juice

salt and white pepper

freshly snipped chives and soured cream, for the garnish

Preheat the grill to high. Cut the chillies in half and discard the seeds. Place in a grill pan, skin-side uppermost, and drizzle with the oil. Grill for 5 minutes, or until the skin has blistered. Remove from the heat and leave to cool.

Discard the skin and membrane from the chillies and roughly chop. Put into a food processor. Peel and seed the avocados, then roughly chop and add to the processor with the stock. Process to a smooth purée.

With the machine still running at low speed, add the cream through the feeder tube, then the milk.

Stir in the lime juice and seasoning to taste. Pour into a soup tureen and chill for at least 1 hour. Serve garnished with snipped chives and soured cream.

HOT-AND-SOUR PRAWN SOUP

Serves 4 to 6

This is a very fragrant soup from Thailand. Some recipes use tamarind to give the sour taste;
others, like this one, use lime juice.

INGREDIENTS

950 ml/34.5 fl oz fish or chicken stock

2 lemongrass stalks

2.5 cm piece of root ginger, peeled and grated

2 or 3 bird's eye (Thai) chillies, seeded and chopped

few fresh kaffir lime leaves

1 large carrot, cut into julienne strips

450 g/1 lb raw large prawns, shelled and deveined

125 g/5 oz wiped and sliced shiitake mushrooms

2 tbsp lime juice

1 tbsp Thai fish sauce

1 tsp chilli paste

200 g/7 oz bean sprouts

2 tbsp freshly chopped coriander

Put the stock into a large pan. Remove the outer leaves from the lemongrass and finely chop. Add to the stock with the ginger, chillies, and lime leaves. Bring to the boil, then reduce the heat and simmer for 10 minutes.

Add the carrot, prawns, and mushrooms to the pan. Simmer for 5 to 8 minutes more, or until the prawns have turned pink.

Mix the lime juice, fish sauce and chilli paste together, then stir into the pan and continue simmering for 1 to 2 minutes. Add the bean sprouts and chopped coriander, stir once and then serve.

FISH SOUP WITH CHILLIES

Serves 4

Use one type of fish for this soup, or a selection. Cod, haddock, red snapper and sea bass are all suitable.

INGREDIENTS

1 tbsp oil

1 large onion, finely chopped

1 garlic clove, crushed

2 celery stalks, trimmed and chopped

2 de agua chillies, seeded and chopped

150 g/6 oz peeled, seeded and chopped tomatoes

1 tbsp tomato purée

450 ml/¾ pint fish stock

450 g/1 lb white fish fillets, skinned and cut into bite-sized pieces

salt and pepper

flat leaf parsley, for the garnish

Heat the oil in a large pan and sauté the onion, garlic, celery and chillies for 5 minutes, or until softened. Add the chopped tomatoes.

Stir in the tomato purée and sauté for 3 minutes more.

Pour in the stock and bring to the boil. Reduce the heat and simmer gently for 10 minutes.

Add the fish and simmer for 5 minutes more, or until the fish is cooked. Season to taste and serve in heated bowls, garnished with flat-leaf parsley.

► *Hot-and-Sour Prawn Soup*

TORTILLA SOUP

Serves 4

This is a typical example of a Mexican 'dry' soup. The name does not mean that there is very little liquid, but rather that the soup contains some sort of dry ingredient, like pasta, rice or even slightly stale tortillas, to absorb some of the stock.

INGREDIENTS

2 tomatoes, halved

2 tbsp olive oil

1 medium onion, chopped

2 garlic cloves

900 ml/32 fl oz chicken stock

lard or oil for deep-frying

12 corn tortillas, preferably a little stale

2 or 3 dried pasilla chillies

salt and pepper

avocado slices and soured cream, for the garnish

Pre-heat the grill. Arrange the tomatoes, cut sides up, in a grill pan. Grill until beginning to brown. Set aside.

Heat half the olive oil in a pan. Add the onion and garlic and sauté for 5 to 7 minutes until softened and golden brown. Tip the contents of the pan into a blender or food processor, add the grilled tomatoes and process to a purée.

Heat the remaining olive oil in the pan and cook the puréed tomato mixture until thick, stirring constantly.

Stir in the stock and bring to the boil, then reduce the heat and simmer for 30 minutes.

While the soup is simmering, heat the lard or oil for deep frying. Cut the tortillas into 5- x 1.75 cm/2- x ½ inch strips. Remove the seeds and veins from the chillies and tear them into pieces. Deep-fry the tortilla strips with the chillies, until the strips are crisp and brown and the chillies are crumbly. Lift out and drain fully on absorbent kitchen paper.

Season the soup. Spoon the crisp tortillas and chillies into heated bowls and ladle the soup on top. Serve at once, garnished with avocado slices and soured cream. Offer lime wedges for squeezing into the soup, if you like.

CHICKEN AND CHILLI SOUP

Serves 4 to 6

This lightly curried soup is quite filling, so serve it solo, with crusty bread, or balance the rest of the meal by following it with a fish dish or main-course salad.

INGREDIENTS

1 tsp oil

1 tsp green curry paste

600 ml/1 pint chicken stock

180 ml/6.5 fl oz coconut milk

1 or 2 bird's-eye (Thai) chillies, seeded and chopped

2 lemongrass stalks, outer leaves removed and finely chopped

4 kaffir lime leaves

2.5 cm piece of root ginger, peeled, and finely grated

325 g/12 oz skinless, boneless chicken breasts, cut into thin strips

175 g/6 oz cut green beans

7.5 cm piece cucumber, peeled if preferred and cut into strips

25 g/1 oz cooked fragrant rice

1 to 2 tsp honey

4 tbsp single cream (optional)

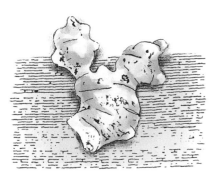

Heat the oil in a large pan and fry the curry paste gently for 3 minutes, stirring occasionally.

Add the stock with the coconut milk, chillies, lemongrass, lime leaves and ginger. Bring to the boil and boil for 3 minutes. Reduce the heat, add the chicken strips and simmer for 5 to 10 minutes, or until the chicken is cooked.

Add the green beans and cucumber with the rice and honey. Simmer for 5 minutes more, or until the vegetables are tender.

Stir in the cream, if using, and serve at once in heated bowls.

CHICKEN AND AVOCADO SOUP

Serves 4

This simple soup comes from Mexico, where it is served in a variety of ways. Chicken and avocado are essential, chillies are optional (but almost always included) and the amount of garlic varies from a single clove to a whole head.

INGREDIENTS

450 ml/¾ pint chicken stock

225 g/8 oz skinless, boneless chicken breast, cut into thin strips

1 or 2 dried red de Arbol chillies

1 to 5 garlic cloves

3 tbsp water

½ to 1 tsp salt

1 avocado

freshly chopped coriander sprigs, for the garnish

Pour the stock into a pan and bring it to the boil; reduce the heat, add the chicken and simmer for 3 to 5 minutes until it is cooked.

Remove the seeds and veins from the chillies. Tear them into pieces and place in a mortar with the garlic and water. Grind to a paste, then sieve into the stock. Stir, simmer for a few minutes and add salt to taste.

Peel the avocado and slice into strips. Separate the slices carefully before dropping them into the soup, or they will stick together. They will sink for a few moments, then float to the surface. When they do, the soup is ready. Serve it in a heated tureen, garnished with coriander.

COOK'S TIP
You can make the soup using cooked chicken. Simply re-heat it in the simmering stock before adding the chilli and garlic paste.

SPICY CHICKEN SOUP

Serves 4

Adding fresh vegetables to this clear chicken soup toward the end of cooking creates a colourful and nutritious dish.
The pepper sauce adds a touch of fire, but don't overdo it or you'll really be going for the burn.

INGREDIENTS

1.5 kg/3 lb chicken

5 garlic cloves, peeled

1 onion, diced

2 celery stalks, including leaves, diced

2 carrots, diced

1 parsnip, diced

1.4 litres/2½ pints water

½ tsp freshly snipped fresh basil

½ tsp curry powder

dash of Hot, Hot, Hot Pepper Sauce
(page 177)

1 tsp freshly chopped coriander

salt and pepper

1 red jalapeño chilli, seeded and thinly
sliced, for the garnish (optional)

Place the chicken in a large pan. Add the whole peeled garlic cloves and half the vegetables. Pour in the water to cover the chicken, then add the basil, curry powder, hot pepper sauce and coriander, with salt and pepper to taste. Bring to the boil, then immediately reduce the heat and simmer uncovered for about 2 hours.

Skim the fat off the top of the soup and strain it into a clean pan. Refrigerate the cooked chicken for later use.

Add the remaining vegetables to the soup. Simmer for 10 minutes more, or until the vegetables are tender. Serve in heated bowls. Garnish with the fresh chilli, if using.

COOK'S TIP
For a more robust soup, add some of the cooked chicken and some noodles or rice.

CALLALOO

Serves 4 to 6

This Caribbean soup takes its name from what is traditionally its chief ingredient, the leaves of the tuberous taro or callaloo plant. Cooks outside the Caribbean have found that fresh spinach, Swiss chard and kale are quite similar to callaloo and a lot easier to track down. Mint green in colour and with a subtle, sharp flavour, the soup makes a refreshing opener for any meal.

INGREDIENTS

225 g/8 oz fresh spinach, Swiss chard or kale

100 g/4 oz okra, sliced (optional)

1 large aubergine, peeled and chopped into bite-sized pieces

900 ml/32 fl oz water

1 tbsp vegetable oil

2 onions, finely chopped

2 garlic cloves, minced

½ tsp thyme

¼ tsp allspice

2 tbsp snipped chives

1 fresh hot chilli, seeded and chopped, or 1 tbsp Tabasco sauce

1 tbsp white wine vinegar

225 ml/8 fl oz coconut milk

Wash and drain the greens, discarding the stems. Chop the leaves into pieces. Place in a large, heavy pan with the okra, if using, and the aubergine.

Add the water and bring to the boil. Reduce the heat and simmer for about 15 minutes until the vegetables are tender. (If you have added okra, check frequently, as this vegetable tends to become glutinous if overcooked.)

Heat the oil in a heavy frying pan and sauté the onions and garlic until the onions are translucent. Add to the pan with the remaining ingredients, and simmer for about 5 minutes more. Purée in a blender or food processor, re-heat if necessary and serve.

RED PEPPER AND CHILLI SOUP

Serves 4

With its glorious colour, this soup makes a great opener for a special meal.

INGREDIENTS

2 red peppers

2 red jalapeño chillies

2 tbsp sunflower oil

1 onion, finely chopped

1 garlic clove, minced

600 ml/1 pint vegetable or chicken stock

225 g/8 oz ripe tomatoes, peeled, seeded, and chopped

salt and pepper

2 tbsp single cream

sliced red pepper, for the garnish

Pre-heat the grill. Cut the peppers and chillies in half, discarding the seeds. Place, skin-side up, on a sheet of aluminium foil in a grill pan. Drizzle with 1 tbsp of the oil and grill for 5 to 10 minutes, or until the skins have blistered. Remove from the heat and place in a bowl. Cover with several pieces of absorbent kitchen paper and leave to cool. When cool, remove the skins from the peppers and chillies and roughly chop the flesh.

Heat the remaining oil in a pan and sauté the onion and garlic for 5 minutes, or until transparent but not browned. Add the chopped peppers and chillies and pour over the stock. Add the tomatoes to the pan, with seasoning to taste. Bring to the boil, then lower the heat, cover and simmer gently for 15 minutes, or until the peppers are really soft.

Leave to cool, then purée in a food processor. If the soup is to be served hot, return it to the rinsed pan, check the seasoning and re-heat gently. If it is to be served cold, chill for at least 1 hour.

To serve, add the cream, and swirl lightly, then sprinkle with a little sliced red pepper.

APPETIZERS

KOREAN CRAB CAKES WITH GINGER DIPPING SAUCE

Serves 4

INGREDIENTS

2 potatoes

1½ garlic cloves, minced

1 fresh red chilli, seeded and finely chopped

2.5 cm/1 in piece root ginger, grated

3 spring onions, finely chopped

375 ml/13 fl oz white and brown crab meat, thawed and drained if frozen

zest of ½ lime

2 tbsp freshly chopped coriander

salt and pepper

1½ tbsp sesame seeds

200 g/2 oz fresh breadcrumbs, for coating

flour for coating

1 egg, beaten

thinly pared cucumber curl and fresh herbs, for the garnish

GINGER DIPPING SAUCE

6 tbsp rice vinegar

2.5 cm/1 in piece root ginger, grated

2 spring onions, white part only, finely chopped

2 tbsp dark soy sauce

2 tsp sugar

Make the sauce by mixing all the ingredients in a small bowl. Set aside.

Cook the potatoes in their skins in boiling water until tender. Drain. When cool enough to handle, peel the potatoes and mash them.

Put the mashed potato in a bowl. Add the garlic, chilli, ginger, spring onions, crab meat, lime peel and coriander. Season well with salt and pepper. Form into eight round cakes about the size of golf balls. Chill for 30 minutes.

Stir the sesame seeds into the breadcrumbs. Spread out on a shallow dish or a sheet of aluminium foil. Have the flour and egg ready in shallow bowls. Coat the crab cakes in the flour, then the egg and finally in the bread crumb mixture, pressing the crumbs on firmly.

Heat the oil for deep-frying to about 170°C/325°F/Gas Mark 3. Fry the crab cakes in batches for about 8 minutes until golden. Transfer to absorbent kitchen paper to drain and keep hot while frying the remaining crab cakes. Serve immediately, garnished with the cucumber curl and fresh herbs. Offer the dipping sauce separately.

COOK'S TIP

Cut a long cucumber in half, then use a vegetable parer to pare off a long, wide ribbon including both flesh and peel. Loop the strip on the plate. Alternatively, garnish the crab cakes with a courgette concertina: head and stem a straight courgette then push a wooden skewer through the centre, right along its length. Rotating the skewer, slice the courgette thinly, then pull the skewer out.

PRAWN RELLENOS

Serves 4

'Rellenos' is a Spanish word meaning stuffed. If tinned chillies are unavailable, use large fresh ones that have been seeded and blanched.

INGREDIENTS

8 to 12 drained tinned large green chillies

225 g/8 oz shelled prawns, finely chopped

4 spring onions, trimmed and chopped

3 green jalapeño chillies, seeded and finely chopped

60 g/2 oz grated hard cheese, such as Cheddar

1 small red apple, cored and finely chopped

grated peel of 1 lemon

salt and pepper

3 to 4 tbsp prepared mayonnaise

salad leaves and sliced red jalapeño chillies, for the garnish

Pat the tinned chillies dry with absorbent kitchen paper and make a slit down one side. Discard the seeds if necessary, then rinse and pat dry again.

Mix the prawns, spring onions, chillies, cheese, apple and lemon peel in a bowl. Add salt and pepper to taste. Stir in the mayonnaise and mix.

Use the prawn mixture to stuff the chillies. Arrange on a serving platter and garnish with salad leaves and thinly sliced red jalapeños.

SCALLOPS WITH HABANERO AND MANGO SLICES

Serves 4

The delicate flavour of the scallops is enhanced, not overwhelmed, by the salsa.

INGREDIENTS

12 large fresh scallops, cleaned

4 tbsp unsalted butter

1 tbsp olive or sunflower oil

assorted bitter salad leaves, such as rocket, endive, radicchio and chicory

edible flowers, such as nasturtiums, for the garnish

SALSA

1 small ripe mango, peeled, stoned and finely chopped

3 spring onions, trimmed and finely chopped

2 orange habanero chillies, seeded and chopped

5 cm/2 in piece cucumber, seeded and finely diced

2 tomatoes, peeled, seeded and finely chopped

1 to 2 tsp demerara sugar or treacle

2 tbsp freshly chopped chervil

Mix all the ingredients for the salsa in a bowl and cover. Chill for 15 minutes. Cut the scallops into thick slices. Rinse, drain and pat dry with absorbent kitchen paper. Heat the butter and oil in a frying pan. When the butter starts to bubble, add the scallops and cook gently for 2 to 3 minutes. Drain. Arrange the salad leaves on a serving platter and top with the scallops. Garnish with the edible flowers and serve.

▶ *Prawn Rellenos*

CRISPY ANCHOVIES

Serves 4

The dried anchovies for this dish are about the size of European whitebait and are deep-fried in the same way. They can be found in most Japanese supermarkets. If the anchovies are very salty, rub or rinse off excess salt before frying. Serve deep-fried anchovies with a sweet/hot sauce to contrast with their saltiness.

INGREDIENTS

1 garlic clove, finely chopped

1 small onion, chopped

1 fresh red chilli, seeded

¾ tsp salt

1½ tsp sugar

2 tbsp vegetable oil, plus extra for deep-frying

about 225 g/4 oz dried anchovies, heads removed if liked, rinsed if necessary

fresh coriander leaves, for the garnish

Combine the garlic, onion, chilli, and salt in a mortar and grind to a paste with a pestle. Stir in the sugar, and set aside.

Heat the 2 tbsp of vegetable oil in a large frying pan. Add the onion paste and cook for 3 to 4 minutes.

Meanwhile, heat the oil for deep-frying to 180°C/350°F/Gas Mark 4. Add the anchovies, in batches if necessary, and fry for 20–30 seconds until very crisp and lightly coloured.

Drain the anchovies on absorbent kitchen paper, then tip into the frying pan and heat through, shaking the pan so that they become coated in the spicy garlic paste. Transfer to a serving bowl, garnish with the coriander leaves and serve at once.

COOK'S TIP
Tossing the fried anchovies with the sauce gives them a wonderful flavour. Offer lime wedges for squeezing, if you like.

MEXICAN MINI-MEATBALLS

Serves 12

These spicy meatballs – albondiguitas – make an excellent appetizer and look very colourful when presented on a platter with a selection of dipping sauces and raw vegetables.

INGREDIENTS

450 g/1 lb lean minced beef

340 g/12 oz ground pork

25 g/1 oz cooked rice

1 small onion, minced

2 garlic cloves, minced

1 red jalapeño chilli, seeded and minced

1 tsp chilli powder, or to taste

2 tsp freshly chopped coriander

salt and pepper

2 eggs, beaten

oil for deep-frying

whole green chillies and olives, for the garnish

crudités and dipping sauces, for serving

Mix the minced beef and pork in a bowl. Add the rice, onion, garlic and chilli, with the chilli powder and coriander. Season with salt and pepper.

Add enough of the beaten egg to bind the mixture, then mix well, using a wooden spoon. Make sure that the onion and chilli are well distributed.

Form the mixture into small rounds, about the size of golf balls, rolling them between the palms of your hands. Make sure your hands are clean.

Heat the oil for deep-frying to 180°C/350°F/Gas Mark 4. Add the meatballs, in batches if necessary, and fry for 4–5 minutes until cooked through. Check by lifting out one of the meatballs and cutting it in half. As soon as a batch of meatballs is cooked, drain on absorbent kitchen paper and keep hot while cooking successive batches.

Pile the meatballs onto a platter and garnish with whole green chillies, ripe and stuffed olives and a selection of crudités. Offer at least two dipping sauces – one mild and one hot, with soured cream or plain yoghurt.

COOK'S TIP
Make larger meatballs, fry them in oil until browned, then poach them in a rich spicy tomato sauce for a delicious family meal. For more sophisticated occasions, hide a pitted olive in the centre of each meatball.

SAUTÉED MUSHROOMS WITH CHILLI SALSA

Serves 4

As easy to eat as they are to prepare, these toast treats make fine appetizers.

INGREDIENTS

6 tbsp virgin olive oil

1 garlic clove, minced

2 de agua chillies, seeded and sliced

2 shallots, thinly sliced

190 g/7.5 oz wiped and sliced assorted wild mushrooms

75 g/3 oz wiped button mushrooms

150 g/6 oz peeled, seeded and chopped plum tomatoes

1 tbsp freshly chopped basil

salt and pepper

1 ciabatta loaf, sliced

Red Chili Sauce (page 175)

sprigs of fresh basil, for the garnish

Heat 4 tbsp of the oil in a frying pan and gently sauté the garlic, chillies, and shallots for 5 minutes, or until the shallots are soft and transparent. Add the mushrooms and continue to cook for 4 to 5 minutes. Stir in the tomatoes, basil and seasoning to taste. Heat through for 1 to 2 minutes.

Meanwhile, drizzle the ciabatta slices with the remaining oil and grill lightly. Arrange the mushroom mixture on the toasted bread, and serve with the chilli sauce. Garnish with sprigs of basil.

CRAB-STUFFED TOMATOES

Serves 4

For an authentic Caribbean flavour, use the fiery pepper sauce recommended, but if you feel this makes the appetizer too hot to handle, use a bottled hot pepper sauce instead.

INGREDIENTS

400 g/14 oz crab meat, thawed and drained if frozen

150 g/5 oz seeded and chopped ripe tomatoes

150 g/5 oz diced seedless cucumber

2 hard-boiled eggs, chopped

150 g/5 oz mayonnaise

Hot, Hot, Hot Pepper Sauce (page 177) to taste

2 tbsp soured cream

2 tsp lime juice

1 tbsp snipped chives

salt and pepper

4 tomatoes

1 soft-leafed lettuce, rinsed and drained

In a bowl, mix together the crab, chopped tomatoes, cucumber and eggs. Cover and chill. In a separate bowl, mix the mayonnaise with the pepper sauce, soured cream, lime juice and chives. Stir in salt and pepper to taste, then cover and chill.

Without cutting all the way through the bottoms, core the whole tomatoes and cut them into sixths, separating the wedges slightly to form tulip shapes. Line four plates with the lettuce, centre a tomato on each and divide the crab mixture among them. Spoon a little of the flavoured mayonnaise over each filled tomato and serve the remaining mayonnaise separately.

▶ *Sautéed mushrooms*

THAI LETTUCE PACKAGES

Serves 4

Good things come in small packages: that is certainly true of these delicious treats.

INGREDIENTS

1 tbsp corn or sunflower oil

1 garlic clove, crushed

2 lemongrass stalks, outer leaves removed and finely chopped

2.5 cm/1 inch piece root ginger, peeled and grated

2 to 3 bird's eye (Thai) red chillies, seeded and chopped

225 g/8 oz shredded skinless, boneless chicken breast

1 tbsp soy sauce

2 tsp Thai fish sauce

200 g/7 oz bean sprouts

1 small Webbs lettuce, separated into leaves

DIPPING SAUCE

2 tbsp Thai fish sauce

2 garlic cloves, crushed

1 to 2 tbsp sugar

2 tbsp lime juice

2 tbsp white wine vinegar

1 bird's eye (Thai) chilli, seeded and finely chopped

Mix all the ingredients for the sauce together in a bowl. Cover and leave for at least 30 minutes for the flavours to develop.

Heat the oil in a wok or large saucepan and stir-fry the garlic, lemongrass, ginger and chillies for 2 minutes.

Add the chicken and continue to stir-fry for 5 minutes, or until the chicken is cooked. Add the soy sauce and fish sauce, stir once, then add the bean sprouts and stir-fry for 30 seconds more.

Arrange a heaped spoonful of the chicken mixture on each lettuce leaf and drizzle with a little of the sauce. Roll up to form a package. Serve the filled packages on a platter, with the remaining dipping sauce.

DEEP-FRIED BRIE WITH SPICY APRICOT SALSA

Serves 4

Deep-fried cheeses are very popular, especially when served with a spicy salsa.

INGREDIENTS

225 g/8 oz Brie cheese

1 large egg, beaten

400 g/8 oz fresh white breadcrumbs

oil for deep-frying

fresh salad leaves, for the garnish

SALSA

1 tbsp sunflower oil

1 small onion, finely chopped

1 red pepper, seeded and finely chopped

1 red fresno chilli, seeded, and finely chopped

200 ml/⅓ pint finely chopped no-need-to-soak dried apricots

180 ml/7 fl oz orange juice

Cut the Brie into four equal portions. Have the beaten egg ready in one shallow bowl and the breadcrumbs in another. Dip the Brie in the beaten egg, then coat in the breadcrumbs. Cover lightly and place in the refrigerator whilst you make the salsa.

Heat the sunflower oil in a pan and gently sauté the onion, red pepper and chilli for 5 minutes. Stir in the apricots and orange juice. Simmer for 15 minutes, or until a chunky consistency is reached.

Heat the oil for deep-frying to 175°C/340°F/Gas Mark 3½ and fry the coated Brie portions for 3 to 4 minutes. Drain on absorbent kitchen paper. Garnish with salad leaves and serve with the apricot salsa.

HOT STUFFED CHILLIES

Serves 4

Chillies play a leading role in this delicious appetizer. Serve with crispy 'seaweed', made by deep-frying shreds of collard greens, then tossing the shreds with a mixture of castor sugar and salt.

INGREDIENTS

450 g/1 lb lean ground pork

1 garlic clove, crushed

1.75 cm/½ inch piece fresh root ginger, peeled and finely chopped

4 spring onions, finely chopped

2 tsp toasted sesame seeds

2 to 3 tsp soy sauce

16 to 20 large fresh red chillies

seasoned flour, for coating

1 large egg, beaten

oil for shallow frying

Mix the pork, garlic, ginger, spring onions, sesame seeds and soy sauce very well.

Cut the chillies in half lengthwise, through the stem and carefully remove the seeds, leaving the chilli 'boats' intact. Break off small pieces of the meat mixture, form into torpedo shapes and use to stuff the chillies, packing the meat mixture in firmly.

Have ready one shallow bowl containing seasoned flour and another containing the beaten egg. Roll the stuffed chillies in the flour to give an even coating, then dip in the egg.

Heat a 1.75 cm/½ inch layer of oil in a frying pan. Add the chillies in batches and fry for 4 to 5 minutes on each side until golden brown and cooked through. Remove from the oil with a slotted spoon and drain on absorbent kitchen paper. Serve hot.

COOK'S TIP
Take care when turning the stuffed chillies over that the filling does not fall out.

FISH AND SEAFOOD

ORANGE- AND CHILLI-MARINATED SARDINES

Serves 4

Sardines cooked this way are simply delicious. Use lime juice instead of orange, if you prefer.

INGREDIENTS

8 to 12 fresh sardines, cleaned

150 ml/¼ pint orange juice

4 tbsp olive oil

4 green jalapeño chillies, seeded and finely sliced

1 tbsp soft light brown sugar

few sprigs of fresh rosemary

orange wedges and sprigs of fresh rosemary, for the garnish

Wipe or lightly rinse the sardines and pat dry with absorbent kitchen paper. Place in a shallow dish. Mix the orange juice, oil, chillies and sugar and pour over the sardines. Tear the sprigs of rosemary into small pieces and scatter over the top. Cover and chill for at least 2 hours, turning the sardines occasionally.

Preheat the grill to medium and line the grill rack with foil. Drain the sardines and place on the foil-lined rack. Grill for 3 to 4 minutes, or until cooked through, basting with the marinade at least once during grilling. Garnish with orange wedges and sprigs of rosemary.

COOK'S TIP
The sardines can be cooked on a barbecue for 3 to 4 minutes once the coals are ready. It is best to place them in a hinged fish grill.

CALYPSO COD STEAKS

Serves 6

These cod steaks have plenty of zip, thanks to the chilli. You can cook salmon in the same way. If you do not have a fresh chilli, use hot-pepper sauce instead.

INGREDIENTS

3 tbsp lime juice

2 tbsp olive oil

2 tsp minced garlic

1 small red chile, seeded, and minced

6 cod or salmon steaks, about 180 g/6 oz each

In a bowl, whisk together the lime juice, olive oil, garlic, and chile.

Brush the grill rack with oil and preheat the grill. Grill the steaks for about 10 to 12 minutes on one side, basting frequently with the sauce, then turn and cook on the other side for 10 to 12 minutes more, again basting frequently, until done. Pour some of the cooking juices over the steaks when serving.

FISH WITH BLACK BEANS

Serves 4

Salted black beans are available in tins from Chinese food stores. They make an excellent marinade and sauce for fish.

INGREDIENTS

900 g/2 lb flounder, whiting or finnan haddie fillet, skinned

3 tbsp salted black beans

90 ml/3.5 fl oz dry sherry

3 tbsp light soy sauce

1 tsp sesame oil

30 g/1 oz cornflour

3 tbsp oil

5 cm/2 inch piece fresh root ginger, peeled and cut in fine strips

1 fresh green chilli, seeded and cut into rings

1 garlic clove, minced

1 piece lemongrass or strip of pared lemon peel

1 bunch green onions, cut diagonally into strips

90 ml/3.5 fl oz water

Cut the fish across into 1.25 cm/½ inch wide strips and place these in a large shallow dish. Sprinkle the salted black beans, sherry, soy sauce and sesame oil over the fish. Cover the dish and leave the strips to marinate for 2 to 3 hours.

When you are ready to cook the fish, drain the strips well, reserving the marinade. Gently toss the strips in the cornflour.

Heat the oil in a wok or frying pan, then stir-fry the ginger, chilli, garlic and lemongrass or peel over medium heat for 4 to 5 minutes to extract their flavour. Add the fish strips to the pan and stir-fry them carefully, avoiding breaking the strips, until they are lightly browned.

Add all the green onions and continue to stir-fry for 2 minutes, until the onions are cooked. Add the water to the reserved marinade and pour the mixture into the wok or frying pan. Bring to the boil over high heat, reduce the heat and stir-fry for 1 minute, then serve.

SQUID WITH HOT PEPPER SAUCE

Serves 4

INGREDIENTS

4 dried ancho chillies

675 g/1½ lb cleaned squid

2 shallots, chopped

2 garlic cloves, crushed

2 red habanero chillies, seeded and chopped

2 tbsp corn or sunflower oil

550 ml/18 fl oz peeled, seeded and chopped plum tomatoes

juice of 2 limes

2 to 3 tsp soft light brown sugar

a few sprigs of fresh oregano

Roast the dried ancho chillies in a non-stick frying pan for 2 to 3 minutes, taking care not to let them scorch. Tip into a bowl and add hot (not boiling) water. Soak for at least 10 minutes, until soft.

Prepare the squid by cutting off the tentacles and rinsing. Remove and discard the head, internal organs and central transparent quill. Rub off the purplish outer skin. Rinse the body, then slice it. Slice the tentacles too.

Put the shallots, garlic, habaneros and drained ancho chillies into a mortar and grind to a paste with a pestle.

Heat the oil in a wok or large pan and gently cook the paste for 3 minutes. Add the tomatoes, lime juice and sugar, and cook for 10 to 12 minutes, or until a thick sauce forms.

Add the oregano, reserving a little for the garnish. Stir in the squid and simmer for 5 minutes, or until the squid is tender. Take care not to overcook, or the squid will become rubbery. Serve sprinkled with the remaining oregano.

YOGHURT-SPICED FISH

Serves 4

INGREDIENTS

4 haddock or cod steaks,
about 175 g/6 oz each, cubed

1 tbsp corn or sunflower oil

2 garlic cloves, crushed

3 red jalapeño chillies, seeded and
finely sliced

1 tsp turmeric

1 tsp ground cumin

1 tsp ground coriander

1 tsp ground fenugreek

6 cardamom pods, crushed

150 g/5 oz plain yoghurt

2 tbsp flaked almonds, toasted

fresh herbs, for the garnish

Place the fish cubes in a shallow dish. Heat the oil in a frying pan and gently sauté the garlic and chillies for 3 minutes, stirring frequently. Add the spices and cook for 3 to 4 minutes more. Turn off the heat, and stir in the yoghurt. Pour the mixture over the fish, then cover and leave to marinate in the refrigerator for at least 1 hour, turning the fish after 30 minutes.

Preheat the grill to medium and line the grill pan with aluminium foil. Drain the fish from the yoghurt mixture and thread onto skewers. Grill for 3 to 4 minutes, or until tender, so the fish flakes easily. Serve sprinkled with the almonds and garnished with fresh herbs.

SALMON STEAKS WITH THAI-STYLE SAUCE

Serves 4

INGREDIENTS

4 salmon steaks, about 175 g/
6 oz each

1 small onion, sliced

2 bay leaves

few sprigs of parsley

4 or 5 black peppercorns

180 ml/6.5 fl oz dry white wine

1 tbsp white wine vinegar

180 ml/6.5 fl oz water

lemon twists, for the garnish

THAI-STYLE SAUCE

2 tbsp olive oil

1 garlic clove, crushed

2.5 cm/1 inch piece root ginger,
peeled and grated

100 g/4 oz shelled raw peanuts

2 red Thai chillies, seeded and sliced

2 tsp soft brown sugar

275 ml/½ pint vegetable stock

1 tbsp lemon juice

Wipe the salmon steaks and set them aside. Place the onion, bay leaves, parsley, peppercorns, wine and vinegar in a frying pan. Add the water and bring to the boil. Reduce the heat and simmer for 10 minutes. Strain and reserve the liquid until you are ready to cook the fish.

Heat the oil for the sauce in the frying pan and sauté the garlic and ginger for 2 minutes. Add the peanuts and fry for 10 minutes, or until golden.

Tip the contents of the frying pan into a food processor and add the chillies, brown sugar, stock and lemon juice. Process to a purée, then scrape into a small saucepan and simmer for 8 to 10 minutes, or until slightly reduced.

Pour the strained spiced vinegar into the cleaned frying pan and add the fish. Bring to the boil, then cover and reduce the heat to a very gentle simmer. Cook for 3 to 4 minutes, or until the fish is cooked. Drain and arrange on serving plates. Spoon a little of the sauce over each portion. Garnish with lemon twists.

STEAMED FISH WITH LEMON AND CHILLI

Serves 4

The combination of lime juice and fresh chillies in the topping give this dish a refreshing spicy tartness.

INGREDIENTS

1 whole sea bass (about 900 g/ 2 lb), cleaned

150 ml/¼ pint lime juice

2 tbsp chopped small fresh green chillies

2 tbsp minced garlic

2 tbsp Thai fish sauce

½ tbsp salt

1 tsp sugar

40 g/1 oz coriander (leaves and cut stems)

lime slices, for the garnish

Steam the fish whole for 20 to 30 minutes until tender but firm. Meanwhile, mix all the remaining ingredients except the coriander in a bowl. When the fish is cooked, place it on a serving platter and immediately spoon the lime juice mixture all over (the fish must be very hot when the sauce is added). Sprinkle with the coriander, garnish with the lime slices and serve.

COOK'S TIP
If you do not have a steamer big enough to hold the fish, sprinkle it lightly with a mixture of lime juice and oil, wrap it in aluminium foil, support it in a roasting tin and cook for about 45 minutes at 180°C/350°F/ Gas Mark 4.

FRIED FISH WITH CHILLI TOPPING

Serves 4 to 6

The scored flesh of the fish traps the spicy sauce, which is poured on top at the last minute.

INGREDIENTS

8 garlic cloves, chopped

5 fresh yellow chillies, chopped

900 g/2 lb whole sea bass, cleaned

½ tsp each salt and ground white pepper

flour for dusting

oil for deep-frying

75 g/2 oz fresh basil leaves

60 ml/2.5 fl oz corn oil

150 ml/¼ pint chicken stock

2 fresh red chillies, quartered lengthwise

1 tbsp tamarind juice or vinegar

2 tsp sugar

1 tsp Thai fish sauce

Put the garlic and yellow chillies in a mortar and pound with a pestle to make a paste.

Score the fish on both sides five or six times, sprinkle on the salt and pepper and dust with the flour. Heat the oil for deep-frying to 180°C/350°F/Gas Mark 4 and fry the fish for 7 to 10 minutes until crisp, but tender inside. Lift out the fish, drain it on absorbent kitchen paper and put it in a serving dish and keep hot. Add the basil leaves to the hot oil and fry for 1 minute until crisp. Drain and reserve for garnishing.

Heat the corn oil in a frying pan and fry the garlic and chilli paste for 1 minute. Add the remaining ingredients and boil lightly for minutes until slightly thick. Pour on top of the fish and sprinkle over with the fried basil.

PRAWNS WITH OKRA

Serves 4

Use baby okra, if you can find them. They will not release as much sap as the larger, sliced pods.

INGREDIENTS

340 g/12 oz okra (prepared weight)
2 tbsp oil
2 onions
2 or 3 whole dried chillies
½ tsp cumin seeds
4 garlic cloves, chopped
¼ tsp turmeric
½ tsp chilli powder
½ tsp ground ginger
3 tomatoes, chopped
225 g/8 oz shelled prawns
1 or 2 fresh green chillies, slit
1 tsp salt
2 tbsp tamarind pulp or lemon juice
2 tbsp freshly chopped coriander

Wash the okra and pat dry with absorbent kitchen paper. Head and stem them, then chop roughly into 1.25 cm/½ inch slices.

Heat the oil in a saucepan and lightly fry the onions with the dried chillies and cumin seeds. Add the garlic, turmeric, chilli powder and ginger. Stir the mixture well and cook for 2 to 3 minutes, stirring continuously.

Add the okra and tomatoes, stirring to coat them well with the spices. Cover the pan and simmer the mixture gently for 5 to 7 minutes, stirring occasionally.

Stir in the prawns with the chillies and the salt. Cook for 5 minutes more, then add the tamarind pulp or lemon juice and coriander leaves. Shake the pan and simmer for 5 minutes more. Then, switch off the heat and let the mixture stand for 2 to 3 minutes before serving.

GOAN PRAWN CURRY

Serves 4

Some of the most delicious spiced dishes are also the simplest. Experiment with the proportions in the spice mix to find the flavour you like most.

INGREDIENTS

3 to 4 whole dried chillies

¼ tsp black peppercorns

½ tsp cumin seeds

1 tsp coriander seeds

2 tbsp grated fresh coconut or dessicated coconut

4 to 5 garlic cloves, chopped

2 tbsp oil

1 onion, finely chopped

2 tsp grated, fresh root ginger

1 to 2 fresh green chillies

1 tsp salt

200 ml/⅓ pint water

2 tbsp tamarind pulp or 1 tbsp vinegar

450 g/1 lb shelled small prawns

2 tomatoes

2 tbsp freshly chopped coriander

few cooked prawns in shells, for the garnish

Crumble the whole dried chillies into a mortar. Add the peppercorns and cumin and coriander seeds and pound with a pestle. Then add the coconut and garlic and pound the mixture again to make a paste.

Heat the oil in a saucepan and fry the onion over low heat. As it begins to turn translucent, add the ginger and green chillies and cook for 30 seconds. Stir in the spice paste, with the salt, and fry for about 1 minute, adding a little of the water if necessary, to thin the mixture.

Add the tamarind pulp or vinegar and stir continuously for 30 seconds.

COOK'S TIP

You can use a coffee grinder to make the paste, but it is best to keep it for spices thereafter, unless you like very spicy coffee!

Stir in the prawns and tomatoes until both are coated in the sauce. Add the remaining water and let the curry cook for 5 minutes over a medium heat.

Add most of the chopped coriander and simmer for 5 to 7 minutes more. Garnish with the remaining coriander and the whole prawns.

STIR-FRIED SQUID WITH CHILLIES AND VEGETABLES

Serves 3 to 4

This is a Korean recipe, and to be truly authentic, you should use the hot, fermented bean paste, *kochujang*, and Korea's excellent coarsely pounded red chilli powder. Korean chili powder adds a characteristic bright, carmine pink colour. A mixture of cayenne pepper and paprika will give a similar result. Chili bean paste can be substituted for the *kochujang*.

INGREDIENTS

560 g/1¼ lb cleaned squid

3 tbsp vegetable oil

1 onion, thinly sliced

2 garlic cloves, minced

1 carrot, thinly sliced lengthwise

1 courgette, thinly sliced lengthwise

2 to 3 long fresh red chillies, thinly sliced lengthwise

2 long fresh green chillies, thinly sliced lengthwise

1 tbsp *kochujang* or chilli bean paste

about ½ tsp Korean chilli powder, or cayenne pepper mixed with paprika

1 tsp sugar

salt and pepper

2 spring onions, white and green parts sliced diagonally

2 tsp sesame oil

toasted sesame seeds, for the garnish

Prepare the squid as described in the recipe for Squid with Hot Pepper Sauce on page 67. Cut open each squid body so that it lies flat, then cut across into 6 ×1.5 cm/2½×½ inch pieces. Cut the tentacles into 6 cm/2½ inch lengths.

Bring a large saucepan of water to the boil. Add all the squid simultaneously and take the pan off the heat. Stir immediately and continue to stir for about 40 seconds, until the squid turns white. Drain well and discard the water.

Heat the oil in a large frying pan over a moderate heat. Add the onion, garlic and carrot. Stir for 30 to 40 seconds, then add the courgette and chillies. Stir in 2 tsp *kochujang* or chilli bean paste, with half the chili powder or cayenne mixture. Stir in the squid with the remaining *kochujang* and chilli powder or cayenne mixture. Add the sugar, and season. Cook over a low heat for 2 minutes, then add the spring onions and sesame oil. Tip into a warm serving dish and garnish with the toasted sesame seeds.

MIXED FISH, CREOLE STYLE

Serves 4

Not surprisingly, chillies and peppers are great companions. Try them in this quick and tasty fish dish.

INGREDIENTS

2 tbsp oil

I large onion, chopped

2 garlic cloves, minced

4 to 5 rocotillo chillies, seeded

2 celery stalks, chopped

I red pepper, seeded and sliced

I green pepper, seeded and sliced

2 tbsp tomato purée

2 tbsp water

fish or chicken stock

400 g/14-oz tin crushed tomatoes

I tsp Worcestershire sauce

salt and pepper

225 g/8 oz white fish fillets,
such as cod

225 g/8 oz mackerel fillets

I tbsp freshly chopped oregano

I tbsp freshly chopped marjoram

juice of ½ lime

100 g/4 oz shelled raw prawns

sprigs of fresh oregano or marjoram,
for the garnish

Heat the oil in a large pan and sauté the onion, garlic, chillies, and celery for 5 minutes. Add the peppers and cook for 3 minutes more.

Mix the tomato purée with the water and stir into the pan with the stock, crushed tomatoes and Worcestershire sauce. Add salt and pepper to taste. Bring to the boil, then reduce the heat and simmer for about 20 minutes, or until the sauce has reduced and is thick.

Skin the fish fillets and discard any bones. Cut the fish into bite-sized pieces. Rinse and pat dry with absorbent kitchen paper.

Add the fish to the pan with the herbs and lime juice. Simmer for 6 minutes more. Add the prawns and cook for 4 minutes more, until the fish flakes easily when tested with the point of a knife.

Garnish with herbs and serve.

SEAFOOD GUMBO

Serves 4

Gumbos vary from region to region; there are no hard and fast rules. One of the staple ingredients is okra, which gives the dish its characteristic texture. The filé powder is used as a thickening agent; flour can be used instead.

INGREDIENTS

2 tbsp corn or sunflower oil

1 large onion, chopped

2 garlic cloves, crushed

2–3 Jamaican hot chillies, seeded and chopped

2 celery stalks, chopped

2 red peppers, seeded and sliced

100 g/4 oz slab bacon, chopped

2 tbsp filé powder or flour

3 smoked pork or Italian sausages, cut into chunks

150 g/6 oz peeled and chopped tomatoes

150 g/6 oz trimmed and sliced okra

600 ml/1 pint chicken stock

225 g/8 oz monkfish, with central bone and skin removed and flesh cubed

225 g/8 oz raw prawns, shelled and deveined

225 g/8 oz squid, prepared (page 67), and sliced

½ to 1 tsp hot pepper sauce

salt and pepper

40 g/1½ oz freshly cooked long-grain rice

2 tbsp freshly chopped parsley

Heat the oil in a large pan and gently sauté the onion, garlic, chillies, and celery for 5 minutes, or until soft.

Add the sliced red peppers and the bacon, and sauté for 3 minutes more. Sprinkle in the filé powder or flour and cook gently for a further 3 minutes.

Add the sausages, tomatoes, okra and stock, then bring to the boil. Reduce the heat and simmer for 10 minutes, stirring occasionally. Add the monkfish and simmer for 10 minutes more, or until the fish is almost tender.

Stir in the prawns, squid and hot pepper sauce, with salt and pepper to taste. Cook for 5 to 7 minutes, or until all the fish is cooked through and flakes easily when tested with the tip of a knife. Be careful not to overcook the squid. Finally add the rice and parsley. Heat through for 5 to 7 minutes and serve.

COOK'S TIP
Use a 275 g/10-oz package of frozen sliced okra instead of fresh, if you like. It will not be necessary to thaw it before adding to the pan.

POULTRY

CHICKEN AND CHILLIES IN SOURED CREAM SAUCE

Serves 4

This is a versatile recipe. You can serve it for a simple supper, with taco chips or hot toast, or dress it up for company by surrounding it with crescents of cooked puff pastry and accompanying it with mange tout and baby carrots.

INGREDIENTS

4 fresh poblano chillies

2 to 3 tbsp lard or olive oil

I large red onion, chopped

450 g/I lb cooked chicken meat, shredded

225 g/8 oz soured cream

115 g/4 oz shredded Cheddar or Monterey Jack cheese

salt and pepper

fresh coriander or parsley, for the garnish

Pre-heat the grill Grill the chillies, turning occasionally, until they are blistered all over. Put them in a bowl, cover with absorbent kitchen paper and set aside whilst you cook the onion.

Heat the lard or oil in a frying pan and sauté the onion for 5 to 7 minutes, until translucent. Peel the chillies, slit them open and remove the seeds and veins. Dice the flesh finely.

Add the chicken and the chillies to the onion. Stir over the heat for about 5 minutes, until both are warm.

Add the soured cream and the shredded cheese, with salt and pepper to taste. Stir continuously over low heat for 2 or 3 minutes, until the cheese melts.

Transfer to a warmed serving dish. Garnish with coriander or parsley and serve immediately.

COOK'S TIP
To make puff pastry crescents, cut circles of puff pastry using a round cutter, then move the cutter across and cut again to make crescents. Brush the crescents with beaten egg and bake in a preheated 200°C/400°F/ Gas Mark 6 oven for about 10 minutes, until golden.

JAMAICAN CHICKEN

Serves 4 to 6

This Caribbean dish incorporates a classic rub – a combination of spices, brown sugar and hot chilli peppers that is applied to the chicken to enliven the dish.

INGREDIENTS

25 g/1½ oz chopped seeded fresh red chillies

4 tsp crushed allspice berries or 1 tsp ground allspice

6 garlic cloves, minced

2 tbsp peeled and chopped fresh root ginger

2 tbsp soft dark brown sugar

60 g/2 oz yellow mustard

1 tsp ground cinnamon

hot pepper sauce, to taste

150 ml/¼ pint olive oil

2 green onions, sliced

60 ml/2.5 fl oz cider vinegar

2 tbsp lime juice

salt and pepper

1.5 kg/3–3½ lb chicken, jointed, 6 large whole legs, or 4 large breasts

Purée the chillies in a blender or food processor. Add the allspice, garlic, ginger, sugar, mustard, cinnamon, hot pepper sauce, olive oil, green onions, vinegar and lime juice. Process until the mixture forms a smooth paste. Add salt and pepper to taste and blend again.

Cut the chicken legs and thighs apart. Cut breasts in half crosswise, leaving the wings attached. Gently lift the skin up from the chicken, exposing the meat, and rub the paste underneath. Then rub into the outside of the skin. Place the pieces on a platter, cover with cling film and refrigerate for 2 hours.

Barbecue or grill the chicken for about 40 minutes at low heat, turning once, until the paste on the skin has formed a dark brown crust.

Alternatively, bake the chicken in a preheated 180°C/350°F/Gas Mark 4 oven for 50 minutes, then transfer to the grill and grill for 2–3 minutes on each side until the skin is dark brown and the paste has formed a crust.

STIR-FRIED CHICKEN

Serves 4

Stir-fries are perennially popular. This one mixes spring onions and dried mushrooms with chillies and peppers.

INGREDIENTS

450 g/1 lb skinless, boneless chicken breasts, cut into strips

2 tbsp soy sauce

1 tbsp sugar

2 spring onions, white and some green parts, finely chopped

2 to 3 fresh green chillies, seeded and minced

1.25 cm/1 inch piece of fresh root ginger, peeled and finely chopped

1½ tsp crushed toasted sesame seeds

freshly ground black pepper

1 small carrot, thinly sliced diagonally

3 dried Chinese black mushrooms, soaked for 30 minutes in hot water

1½ tbsp sesame oil

1 red pepper, seeded and cut into thin strips

FRIED EGG STRIP GARNISH

vegetable oil, for frying

1 egg, lightly beaten

Spread out the chicken strips in a shallow bowl. In a separate bowl, mix the soy sauce, sugar, spring onions, chillies, ginger, sesame seeds and plenty of pepper. Pour over the chicken, turning to coat the strips. Cover and let stand for 30 minutes.

Meanwhile, bring a small pan of water to the boil and cook the carrot slices for 5 minutes. Drain and set aside.

Drain the mushrooms. Cut out and discard any hard patches and the stalks. Slice the mushrooms caps.

Make the garnish. Heat a thin film of oil in a large non-stick frying pan or wok. Add the beaten egg, tilting the pan so that it forms a thin, even layer. Fry the omelette for 1 to 2 minutes until set, then flip over and fry the other side. Slide the omelette onto a board, roll it up and cut it into thin strips. Set aside.

Heat the sesame oil in a wok or frying pan. Drain the chicken, reserving the marinade, and add it to the pan. Stir-fry for 2 to 3 minutes. Lift out of the pan and set aside. Add the mushrooms and carrots to the oil remaining in the pan and stir-fry for 2 minutes, then add the pepper and stir-fry for 1 minute more.

Return the chicken to the pan. Add the reserved marinade and bring to a boil. Stir and cook for 1 minute, then serve garnished with egg strips.

CHILLI CHICKEN WITH PINE NUTS

Serves 4

INGREDIENTS

1 tbsp sunflower oil

1 tbsp butter

4 chicken portions

225 g/4 oz slab lean bacon, trimmed and cubed

1 onion, sliced

1 garlic clove, crushed

4 green fresno chillies, seeded and sliced

25 g/1 oz all-purpose flour

450 ml/¾ pint chicken stock

grated peel of 1 lemon

salt and pepper

135 g/5 oz whole-kernel corn

2 tbsp freshly chopped parsley

3 tbsp pine nuts, toasted

Preheat the oven to 190°C/ 375°F/Gas Mark 5. Heat the oil and butter in a frying pan and seal the chicken portions and bacon cubes on all sides. Drain and place in a large oven-proof casserole dish.

Add the onion, garlic and chillies to the frying pan and gently sauté for 5 minutes, or until softened. Sprinkle in the flour and cook, stirring constantly, for 2 minutes. Gradually add the stock, then bring to the boil. Add the lemon peel with salt and pepper to taste.

Pour the onion mixture over the chicken and bacon, cover the casserole dish and cook for 40 minutes. Remove from the oven and stir in the corn. Cook for 15 minutes more, or until the chicken portions are cooked through. Stir in the parsley and pine nuts, and serve.

CHICKEN KEBABS WITH CHILLI SAUCE

Serves 4

Marinated chicken strips, threaded on wooden skewers and grilled, taste absolutely delicious with a
chilli and peanut sauce.

INGREDIENTS

275 g/10 oz skinless, boneless chicken
breast, skinned

chopped chilli, for the garnish

MARINADE

2 shallots, finely chopped

1 garlic clove, crushed

4 Thai red chillies, seeded and
chopped

5 cm piece root ginger,
peeled and grated

2 tbsp soy sauce

2 tsp honey, warmed

2 tbsp lemon juice

CHILI SAUCE

1 Thai red chilli,
seeded and finely chopped

1 tbsp lime juice

60 ml/2.5 fl oz Thai fish sauce

1 tbsp roasted peanuts, finely crushed

2 spring onions,
trimmed and finely shredded

If using wooden skewers, soak them in cold water for 1 hour so that they do not scorch in the grill.

Cut the chicken breasts into narrow 7.5 × 1.25 cm/3 × ½ inch strips, and place in a shallow dish. Combine all the marinade ingredients in a bowl and pour over the chicken strips. Turn to ensure they are well coated. Cover the dish and chill for at least 3 hours, turning the chicken occasionally in the marinade.

Meanwhile, prepare the chilli sauce. Mix all the ingredients in a small pan and heat through, stirring occasionally. Keep hot until required.

Pre-heat the grill to medium-high. Drain the chicken, reserving the marinade, and thread onto the wooden skewers.

Brush the chicken strips with a little of the reserved marinade and grill for 8 to 10 minutes, brushing occasionally with more marinade and turning the kebabs several times, until the chicken is cooked. Garnish with the chopped chilli, and serve with the sauce.

ARROZ CON POLLO

Serves 4

The title simply means rice with chicken, but the reality is considerably more exciting. In Mexico, where the dish is extremely popular, chillies add a fiery note, and the dish resembles a spicy paella.

INGREDIENTS

3 tbsp olive or sunflower oil

4 chicken portions, cut in half

1 Spanish onion, chopped

2 garlic cloves, crushed

5 red Anaheim chillies, seeded and sliced

400 g/14 oz risotto rice

few strands of saffron

600–875 ml/1 pint to 1½ pints chicken stock

salt and pepper

100 g/4 oz raw shelled prawns

135 g/5 oz shelled peas

135 g/5 oz cut green beans

450 g/1 lb fresh mussels, scrubbed, beards removed and any open ones discarded

lemon wedges and flat-leaved parsley, for the garnish

Heat the oil in a paella or large frying pan and brown the chicken on all sides. Lift out of the pan and drain on absorbent kitchen paper.

Add the onion, garlic and chillies to the oil remaining in the pan and sauté for 5 minutes. Stir in the rice and saffron. Cook, stirring occasionally, for 3 minutes more.

Return the chicken to the pan and stir in 450 ml of the stock, with salt and pepper to taste. Bring to the boil, then lower the heat and simmer for 20 minutes, adding more stock as necessary.

Add the prawns, vegetables and mussels to the pan with extra stock if required. Cook for 8 to 10 minutes more, or until the rice is tender and the chicken is cooked. Discard any mussels that have not opened. Check the seasoning, garnish with the lemon wedges and parsley and serve.

SPATCHCOCKED CHICKEN WITH CHILLI SAUCE

Serves 4

Spatchcock the chicken by placing it breast-down and splitting it in half with a cleaver, without cutting clear through to the breast. Open the carcass out, turn it over and flatten it.

INGREDIENTS

10 garlic cloves, finely chopped

2 tbsp black peppercorns, crushed

2 tbsp light soy sauce

2 tbsp sugar

2 tbsp brandy

1 tsp salt

1.5 kg/3 lb whole chicken, spatchcocked

tomato peel roses and lettuce leaves, for the garnish

SAUCE

225 ml/8 fl oz white vinegar

115 g/4 oz sugar

3 garlic cloves, roughly chopped

2 fresh red chillies, pounded well

½ tbsp salt

Mix the garlic, peppercorns, soy sauce, sugar, brandy and salt in a dish that will hold the flattened chicken. Add the bird, spoon the marinade over it and marinate for 3 to 4 hours. Pre-heat the oven to 180°C/350°F/Gas Mark 4. Put the chicken in a roasting tin, brush with a little of the marinade and roast for 40 minutes, turning the bird halfway through. Meanwhile, mix all the sauce ingredients in a pan and boil until thick. Leave to cool.

Garnish the chicken with roses shaped from pared tomato peel, and lettuce leaves. Serve with the sauce.

CHILLI-TEQUILA CHICKEN WINGS

Serves 4

Chilli spices season the chicken wings, whilst tequila and citrus juices tenderize them. These are delicious served on their own or with other barbecued foods.

INGREDIENTS

3 dried chipotle chillies

5 garlic cloves, chopped

juice of 2 limes

juice of 1 orange

2 tbsp tequila

1 tbsp mild chilli powder

2 tbsp vegetable oil

1 tsp sugar

¼ tsp ground allspice

pinch of ground cinnamon

pinch of ground cumin

pinch of dried oregano, crumbled

salt and pepper

12 to 16 chicken wings

Roast the dried chipotle chillies in a non-stick frying pan for 2 to 3 minutes, taking care not to let them scorch. Tip into a bowl and add hot (not boiling) water. Soak for at least 10 minutes until soft, then purée in a blender or a mortar and pestle.

In a large shallow dish, mix the chillies with all the remaining ingredients except the chicken. Season well.

Add the chicken wings and turn to coat them in the mixture. Cover and marinate for at least 3 hours, preferably overnight.

Grill over medium coals for 15 to 20 minutes or until the wings are crisply browned and cooked through.

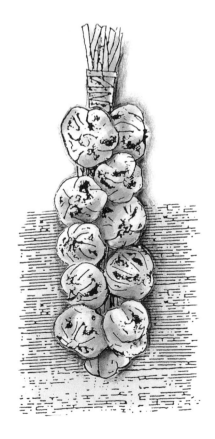

BARBECUED CHICKEN WINGS

Serves 4

Everyone's favourite – barbecued chicken wings are so good that it always makes sense to cook double the quantity.

INGREDIENTS

12 to 16 chicken wings

Green Chili Sauce (page 174), tossed green salad and warm bread, to serve

MARINADE

2 tbsp sunflower oil

2 tbsp soft dark brown sugar

2 tbsp soy sauce

150 ml/¼ pint orange juice

2 garlic cloves, crushed

4 red jalapeño chillies, seeded and sliced

Wipe the chicken wings and trim them if necessary. Place in a single layer in a large shallow dish.

Mix all the marinade ingredients together in a pan and heat through, stirring occasionally, until the sugar has dissolved. Bring to the boil and boil for 5 minutes. Let cool slightly, then pour over the chicken wings. Turn the wings to ensure they are well coated, then cover the dish and leave in a cool place for at least 3 hours. Turn the wings or spoon the marinade over the chicken occasionally.

If you plan to use wooden skewers to hold the wings, soak them in cold water for 1 hour so that they do not scorch on the barbecue.

Drain the chicken wings, reserving a little of the marinade, and thread onto the skewers. Place on the barbecue grill and brush with the reserved marinade. Cook over medium coals for 15 to 20 minutes, turning occasionally and brush with the reserved marinade until the wings are cooked. Serve with the chilli sauce, salad and bread.

SPICED CHICKEN WITH GREEN PEPPER

Serves 4

This simple stir-fry owes its superb flavour to the combination of sauces added at the end.

INGREDIENTS

60 ml/2.5 fl oz corn oil

1 tbsp chopped garlic

325 g/11 oz skinless, boneless chicken breasts, cut lengthwise into 1.25 cm/½ inch slices

100 g/4 oz sliced green pepper

5 fresh red chillies, sliced lengthwise

1 onion, thickly sliced

1 tbsp oyster sauce

½ tbsp light soy sauce

1 tsp fish sauce

¼ tsp dark soy sauce

basil leaves

cooked rice, for serving

Heat the oil in a wok or pan, add the garlic and chicken and fry well for 1 minute. Add the green pepper and chiles, mix, then add the onion and cook for 1 minute. One by one stir in the sauces, cooking for about 30 seconds after each addition. Check that the chicken is cooked through, then stir in the basil. Remove from the heat immediately after stirring in the basil and serve the stir-fry with rice.

COOK'S TIP

It is a good idea to preheat a wok for a few seconds before adding any oil for stir-frying. Add the oil in an even drizzle around the top of the wok – bracelet-style – so that it slides down to coat the entire inner surface. You do not need to use much oil. Give it a few seconds to heat before adding the food.

CHICKEN WITH CHICKPEAS

Serves 4

Chickpeas – or garbanzos, as they are also known – make a wonderful addition to spiced dishes. If you use dried chickpeas, rather than tinned, soak them in water overnight and cook them for 1½ to 2 hours, until tender, before adding them to the pan.

INGREDIENTS

450 g/1 lb skinless, boneless chicken breasts, cut into 2.5 cm/1 inch cubes

1 onion, chopped

2 tomatoes, 1 chopped, 1 sliced

1 garlic clove, minced

2 tsp minced fresh root ginger, plus 1 tsp fresh root ginger cut into very fine matchstick strips

1 tsp salt

1 tsp chilli powder

¼ tsp turmeric

½ tsp Garam Masala

1 tbsp oil

drained tinned chickpeas (garbanzos)

about 225 ml/8 fl oz water

1 to 2 fresh green chillies

½ tsp cumin seeds, crushed

3 tbsp freshly chopped coriander leaves, or chopped spring onions for the garnish

2 tsp lemon juice

Put the chicken into a heavy saucepan. Add the onion and the chopped tomato, then stir in the garlic and the minced ginger. Sprinkle over with the salt. Cook over a low heat for 10 minutes or until the chicken releases its moisture, stirring occasionally.

Add the chilli powder, turmeric and garam masala and cook for 10 to 15 minutes more.

Add the oil and cook the mixture uncovered until almost all the moisture has evaporated and the chicken and vegetables look slightly glazed.

Add the chickpeas and green chillies. Mix them in well, then add the water. Bring it to the boil then lower the heat and simmer for 7 to 8 minutes.

Lastly, add the cumin seeds, ginger strips, coriander and lemon juice. Simmer for a couple more minutes, then garnish the dish with tomato slices, coriander or chopped spring onions.

CHICKEN IN RED CHILLI AND TOMATO SAUCE

Serves 4

As colourful as it is good to eat, this is sure to prove popular with family and friends.

INGREDIENTS

6 dried ancho chillies, roasted

1.25 kg/2½ lb chicken

2 onions

1 carrot, roughly chopped

3 bay leaves

2 garlic cloves

4 tbsp sesame seeds, toasted

½ tsp ground cinnamon

½ tsp ground cloves

1 tbsp sunflower oil

400 g/14-oz can crushed tomatoes

1 tbsp tomato purée

1 tbsp freshly chopped oregano

salad and warm bread, to serve

Re-hydrate the roasted chillies by soaking them in hot water for 10 minutes. Place the chicken in a large pan with one of the onions, the carrot and the bay leaves. Cover with cold water and bring to the boil. Skim off any foam that rises to the surface. Cover the pan with a lid and simmer for 1½ hours, or until the chicken is tender and fully cooked.

Let the chicken cool, then remove the cooked chicken meat from the carcass, discarding the skin, and cut into thin strips. Reserve 1½ pints of the cooking liquid.

Drain the chillies and put them in a food processor. Chop the remaining onion and add it to the chiles with the garlic, sesame seeds and spices. Process with a little of the reserved stock to make a smooth paste.

Heat the oil in a frying pan and cook the paste gently for 2 minutes. Add the chopped tomatoes, tomato purée and remaining stock. Bring to the boil, reduce the heat and simmer for 10 minutes.

Add the chicken to the pan and simmer for 10 to 15 minutes more, or until the chicken is piping hot. Sprinkle with the chopped oregano and serve.

VIETNAMESE GRILLED CHICKEN

Serves 4

If preferred, bird's-eye (Thai) chillies can be substituted for the dried chillies. Depending on your heat tolerance, you should use 1 to 3 bird's-eye (Thai) chillies instead of the dried ancho chillies.

INGREDIENTS

6 dried ancho chillies, roasted and seeded

2 lemongrass stalks, outer leaves removed and chopped

2 garlic cloves, crushed

5 cm/2 inch piece root ginger, peeled and grated

100 g/4 oz chopped onions

1 tbsp soft dark brown sugar

1 tsp turmeric

2 tbsp sunflower oil

4 chicken portions, cut in half

flat-leaved parsley, lemon wedges and sliced green chillies, for the garnish

Re-hydrate the roasted chillies by soaking them in hot water for 10 minutes. Drain, then put the chillies into a food processor with the lemongrass, garlic, ginger, onions, sugar and turmeric. Blend to form a thick, chunky paste.

Heat the oil in a frying pan and cook the paste, stirring constantly, for 2 minutes. Remove from the heat, let cool slightly and brush over the chicken portions. Cover the chicken and leave in a cool place for at least 3 hours.

Pre-heat the grill to medium-high. Place the chicken on the grill rack lined with aluminium foil and grill, turning occasionally, for 15 minutes, or until the chicken is tender and the juices run clear. Serve garnished with flat-leaved parsley, lemon wedges and slices of green chillies.

MARINATED GRILLED CHICKEN

Serves 4

Probably better known as Chicken Tikka, this is one of the most popular choices on Indian restaurant menus. It is easy to make, and when prepared by the method below, it is a low-fat dish.

INGREDIENTS

4 skinless, boneless chicken breasts

1 large onion, chopped

2 garlic cloves, minced

1 tbsp minced fresh root ginger

2 fresh green chillies, roughly chopped

2 tbsp plain yoghurt

½ to 1 tsp chilli powder

½ tsp garam masala

¼ tsp ground mace

1 tbsp lemon juice

freshly chopped coriander

½ tsp salt

Score the chicken breasts diagonally across in 3 to 4 places.

Combine the remaining ingredients in a blender or food processor and process to a smooth paste. Spread the spice paste over the chicken pieces, rubbing it in well. Cover the chicken and refrigerate for at least 3 hours, preferably overnight.

Pre-heat the grill to high and line the grill pan with aluminium foil. Grill the chicken breasts under the hot grill for 4 to 5 minutes, then reduce the heat and continue cooking for another 15 to 20 minutes, turning them over halfway through.

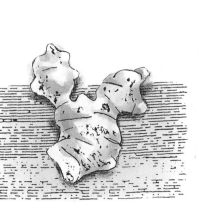

CHICKEN FRIED WITH CASHEW NUTS

Serves 4

Chicken and cashews are a timeless combination. Chillies give the dish a bit of zip.

INGREDIENTS

325 g/11 oz skinless, boneless chicken breasts, cut into slices

flour for coating

225 ml/8 fl oz corn oil

4 dried red chillies, fried and cut into 1.25 cm/½ inch pieces

1 tbsp chopped garlic

10 spring onions, white parts only, cut into 5 cm pieces

35 g/5 oz unsalted cashew nuts, roasted

1 onion, sliced

2 tbsp oyster sauce

1 tbsp light soy sauce

dash of dark soy sauce

1 tbsp sugar

Coat the chicken breasts lightly with flour. The easiest way to do this is to put the flour in a strong plastic bag and add the chicken slices. Shake the bag until the slices are evenly coated, then lift them out, leaving the excess flour behind. Heat the oil in a pan or wok and stir-fry the chicken for about 5 minutes until light brown. Remove almost all the oil from the pan.

Add the chiles and garlic to the chicken in the pan and fry for 1 minute. Add the scallions, cashews, and onion and stir-fry for 3 minutes.

Stir in the sauces and sugar and cook for 1 or 2 minutes, until the chicken and vegetables are glazed. Serve immediately.

COOK'S TIP

If you prefer a milder chilli flavour, leave the chillies whole and either remove them before serving or give guests the choice of whether to leave them in or take them out.

DUCK IN GREEN CHILLI SAUCE

Serves 4

Arrowroot is used to thicken the sauce without muddying the colour, but cornflour can be used instead.

INGREDIENTS

4 green serrano chillies, seeded and sliced	2 tbsp freshly chopped coriander
150 g/6 oz seeded and chopped tomatillos or green tomatoes	2 tsp honey
1 onion, chopped	salt and pepper
2 garlic cloves, chopped	1 tbsp arrowroot
grated peel of ½ lemon, if using green tomatoes	1 tbsp water
	4 duck breasts
180 ml/6.5 fl oz chicken stock	Red Chilli Sauce (page 175) for serving
	coriander sprigs, for the garnish

Pre-heat the grill to medium-high. Put the chillies, tomatillos or tomatoes, onion, garlic and lemon peel, if using, into a food processor. Process to a purée, then sieve into a pan. Gradually stir in the stock.

Heat the chilli mixture gently for 4 minutes, stirring occasionally. Stir in the coriander and honey, with salt and pepper to taste.

Mix the arrowroot with the water, stir into the pan and cook, stirring constantly, until the sauce thickens and clears. Keep warm.

Wipe the duck breasts, discard any excess fat and prick the skin with a fork. Season with salt and pepper.

Place the duck breasts, skin side up, in a grill pan. Grill, turning at least once, for 25 minutes, or until cooked to personal preference.

To serve, pour a little of the chilli sauce onto each serving plate. Slice the duck breasts. Arrange in a fan shape with the chilli sauce and serve extra sauce separately. Garnish with coriander sprigs.

DUCK BREASTS WITH PUMPKIN SEEDS

Serves 4

The pumpkin seeds in the chilli sauce are used to thicken and flavour. Mexican cooks also use sesame seeds and pine nuts for the same purpose.

INGREDIENTS

4 duck breasts, about 150 g/6 oz each

SAUCE

35 g/1.5 oz pumpkin seeds, toasted
2 tbsp sunflower oil
1 small onion, chopped
3 or 4 green fresno chillies, seeded and chopped
2 garlic cloves, chopped
chicken stock
1 tbsp freshly chopped coriander
¼ tsp salt
200 g/8 oz chopped fresh spinach

Make the sauce. Reserve a few of the pumpkin seeds for the garnish; finely grind the remainder.

Heat the oil in a pan and gently sauté the onion, chillies, and garlic for 3 minutes. Add the stock and simmer for 1 minute. Stir in the ground pumpkin seeds, coriander, salt and spinach and simmer for 3 minutes more. Remove from the heat and keep warm.

Pre-heat the grill to high and line the grill pan with aluminium foil.

Prick the skin on the duck breasts with a fork and place, skin-side uppermost, in the grill pan. Grill for 2 minutes on each side, then reduce the temperature of the grill to medium-hot and turn the duck breasts over. Continue grilling for 15 to 20 minutes, turning at least once, until the duck is cooked to personal preference. Serve the duck breasts, sprinkled with the reserved pumpkin seeds. Serve the sauce separately.

DUCK WITH TWO SAUCES

Serves 4

A very popular dish of Chinese origin, with two contrasting sauces.

INGREDIENTS

1.75 kg/4 lb roasting duck

red food colouring

200 g/8 oz hot boiled rice

4 tbsp thinly sliced pickled ginger

4 tbsp thinly sliced sweet dill pickle

COOKED SAUCE

450 ml/¾ pint chicken stock

1 tbsp sugar

½ tbsp light soy sauce

1 tsp dark soy sauce

1 tsp flour

SOY CHILLI SAUCE

150 ml/¼ pint dark soy sauce

3 fresh red chillies, sliced thinly into circles

1 tbsp sugar

½ tbsp vinegar

Pre-heat the oven to 200°C/400°F/Gas Mark 6. Wipe the duck inside and out, discarding any excess fat from the cavity. Prick the skin all over with a fork, then rub it with red food colouring. Roast the duck on a rack over a roasting tin for 1¾ to 2 hours, until fully cooked. Remove the flesh and cut it into 6.5 x 1.5 cm/2½ x ½ inch slices. Keep hot.

Heat the ingredients for the cooked sauce together in a pan and boil for 1 minute. Mix the ingredients for the soy chilli sauce in a bowl.

Divide the rice among four serving plates, and arrange the duck meat over the top. Spoon the cooked sauce over these and garnish with the ginger and pickle slices. Serve the soy chilli sauce separately.

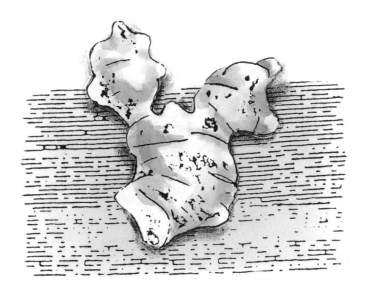

ROAST DUCK WITH CHILLIES

Serves 4

Roast duck with a chilli rub makes an unusual dish, especially when served with the spicy salsa.

INGREDIENTS

1.75 kg/4 lb roasting duck

4 red serrano chillies, seeded and finely chopped

2 tbsp soft dark brown sugar

1 tsp salt

1 tsp ground cinnamon

½ tsp ground cloves

zest of 1 lime

lime zest and flat-leaved parsley, for the garnish

SALSA

150 g/6 oz peeled, seeded and finely chopped ripe tomatoes

6 spring onions, finely chopped

1 passionfruit (grenadilla) halved, with the seeds removed

2 red serrano chillies, seeded and finely chopped

Wipe the duck, inside and out, discarding any excess fat from the cavity. Prick the skin all over with a fork. Mix the chillies, sugar, salt, cinnamon, cloves and lime zest in a bowl. Sprinkle the inside of the duck with 1 tbsp of the mixture and use the remainder to rub all over the duck skin. Leave in a cool place for at least 4 hours.

Make the Salsa. Combine all the ingredients in a bowl. Set aside to let the flavours develop.

At least 15 minutes before roasting the duck, preheat the oven to 200°C/400°F/Gas Mark 6. Place the duck on a trivet or rack standing in a roasting tin. Roast for 1¾ to 2 hours, or until the duck is tender and the juices run clear when the thickest part of a thigh is pierced with a skewer.

Garnish the cooked duck with lime zest and flat-leaved parsley, and serve with the salsa.

WHITE CHILLI WITH CHICKEN

Serves 6

This is a low-fat, moderately spicy chilli, made with chicken, white beans and Anaheim chillies.

INGREDIENTS

400 g/14 oz white beans, picked over and soaked overnight

1 tbsp chilli powder

½ tsp ground cumin

½ tsp dried thyme

½ tsp dried oregano

½ tsp cayenne pepper

½ tsp garlic powder

1 tbsp flour

3 boneless, skinless chicken breasts, cut into 1.25 cm/½ inch cubes

2 tbsp vegetable oil

1 onion, chopped

1 celery stalk, chopped

450 ml/¾ pint chicken stock

4 Anaheim chillies, roasted, peeled and chopped, or a 100 g/4-oz can chopped green chillies

about 1 tsp salt

30 g/1 oz freshly chopped coriander

Drain the beans, put them in a large pan and barely cover with fresh water. Bring to the boil, boil hard for 5 minutes, then reduce the heat to a simmer.

Mix the spices, herbs, seasonings and flour in a strong plastic bag. Add the chicken cubes and toss until they are evenly coated with the spice mix. Set aside.

Heat 1 tablespoon of the oil in a frying pan and sauté the onion and celery for 6 minutes. Add the vegetables to the beans.

Heat the remaining oil in the cleaned frying pan and cook the chicken, turning often, until all sides are lightly browned. Add the chicken to the beans with the chicken stock and chillies. Simmer for about 1½ hours, until the beans are tender, adding water or chicken stock if the chilli looks too dry. Add salt to taste. Sprinkle in the coriander just before serving.

GROUND TURKEY CHILLI WITH BLACK BEANS

Serves 4 to 6

Set your tastebuds sizzling with this hot and spicy chilli.

INGREDIENTS

2 dried ancho chillies

2 dried Anaheim chillies

225 ml/8 fl oz boiling water

450 g/1 lb minced turkey

225 ml/8 fl oz chicken stock

2 tbsp vegetable oil

1 medium onion, chopped

1 celery stalk, chopped

2 fresh jalapeño or serrano chillies, unseeded, minced

400 g/14-oz tin chopped tomatoes

¼ tsp dried sage

1 tsp dried oregano

425 g/15-oz tin black beans

about 1 tsp salt

Cut the dried chillies in half and remove the stems and seeds. Put them in a small heat-proof bowl. Pour the boiling water over the chillies, making sure all parts are immersed. Let chillies soak for about 30 minutes while you prepare the other ingredients.

Brown the minced turkey in a non-stick frying pan, stirring to break up any large lumps. Drain fat, if needed. Put the turkey in a large saucepan and add the chicken stock. Bring to simmering point.

Heat the oil in the cleaned frying pan and sauté the onion and celery for 5 minutes. Tip the contents of the frying pan into the pan and add the fresh chillies, tinned tomatoes, sage and oregano. Bring to the boil, then lower the heat and let the turkey mixture simmer.

Pour the dried chillies and their water into a blender or food processor. Purée until a thick red sauce forms. Strain the sauce and discard the solids. Add the sauce to the turkey mixture and simmer for 15 minutes, adding water or chicken stock if needed. Stir in the beans, with salt to taste. Heat through and serve.

TURKEY IN CHOCOLATE SAUCE

Serves 4

Don't be put off by the title – the only evidence of chocolate in this classic Mexican dish is in the richness of the sauce.

INGREDIENTS

3 dried ancho chillies

3 dried pasilla chillies

3 dried mulato chillies

1 onion, chopped

2 garlic cloves, minced

4 tbsp sesame seeds, toasted

2 tbsp flaked almonds, toasted

1 tsp ground coriander

½ tsp freshly ground black pepper

a few cloves

3 to 4 tbsp sunflower oil

275 ml/½ pint chicken stock

300 g/3 oz peeled, seeded and chopped tomatoes

2 tsp ground cinnamon

50 g/1.5 oz raisins

50 g/2 oz pumpkin seeds, toasted

2 oz unsweetened chocolate, melted

1 tbsp red wine vinegar

8 turkey thigh portions or 2 skinless, boneless chicken breasts

fresh herbs, for the garnish

Roast the dried chillies in a non-stick frying pan for 2 to 3 minutes, taking care not to let them scorch. Tip into a bowl and add hot (not boiling) water. Soak for at least 10 minutes until soft, then drain, reserving the soaking liquid.

Put the re-hydrated chillies in a food processor and add the onion, garlic and half the sesame seeds, with the almonds, coriander, black pepper and cloves. Grind to form a paste.

Heat 2 tbsp of the oil in a heavy pan and gently cook the paste for 5 minutes, stirring frequently.

Add 180 ml/6.5 fl oz of the stock, the tomatoes, cinnamon, raisins and pumpkin seeds. Bring to the boil, then reduce the heat and simmer for 15 minutes, or until a thick consistency is reached. Stir in the melted chocolate and vinegar, mixing well. Cover the pan and keep the mixture warm until needed.

Heat the remaining oil in a frying pan and seal the turkey thighs or chicken breasts on all sides. Drain off the oil and add the remaining stock. Bring to the boil, then reduce the heat and simmer for 15 minutes, or until tender. Drain off any liquid.

Pour the sauce over the turkey or chicken and re-heat gently. Sprinkle over with the remaining toasted sesame seeds and garnish with fresh herbs.

COOK'S TIP
Use a mortar and pestle to make the chilli paste if you prefer.

MEAT DISHES

BISTECK RANCHERO

Serves 4

This is a traditional Mexican way of cooking steak. As is often the case in Mexican cooking, the steak is served well done, having first been pan-fried, and then smothered with vegetables and chillies and cooked in the covered frying pan.

INGREDIENTS

1½ tbsp vegetable oil

675 g/1½ lb very thinly sliced beef steak

1 onion, thickly sliced

2 beefsteak tomatoes, chopped or sliced

2 green California chillies, seeded and sliced

3 to 4 serrano chillies, seeded and chopped

4 tbsp chicken stock

whole trimmed spring onions, halved tomatoes and stuffed green olives, to garnish

Refried Beans (page 26) and side salad, for serving

Heat the oil in a large frying pan. Pan-fry the steak over high heat for 2 minutes on each side. Smother with the onion slices, chopped tomatoes and chillies.

Pour over the stock, cover the frying pan tightly and reduce the heat. Cook for about 15 minutes or until the steak is tender.

Garnish each portion with a spring onion and half a tomato topped with a stuffed olive. Add a portion of refried beans to one side of the plate and a side salad to the other.

BEEF HOTPOT WITH CHILLI MARINADE

Serves 4 to 6

In Korea, where this recipe originated, the hotpot is a communal one-pot meal prepared over a burner at the table. Everyone dips into the pot to select their chosen morsels. Any number of a wide variety of ingredients can be added, according to what is available, or to suit the occasion.

INGREDIENTS

550 g/1¼ lb sirloin or fillet steak, partly frozen

750 ml/25 fl oz brown veal or chicken stock

6 celery stalks, cut into 5 cm/2 inch pieces

2 young carrots, finely sliced diagonally

8 crimini mushrooms

8 spring onions, cut diagonally into 5 cm/2 inch pieces

6 Chinese leaves, cut into 5 cm/2 inch pieces

1½ × 100 g/4-oz cakes of bean curd, cut into 2.5 cm/1 inch cubes

MARINADE

2 tsp sesame seeds

3 tbsp sugar

1 fresh red chilli, seeded and finely chopped

6 tbsp soy sauce

1 plump garlic clove, minced

COOK'S TIP
If you cook this in a fondue pot at the table, boil the stock in a saucepan before adding it to the seared meat.

Make the marinade. Heat a heavy non-stick frying pan, add the sesame seeds and toast until pale brown. Remove and crush finely. Tip into a bowl and stir in the remaining marinade ingredients.

Slice the beef and cut into 1 × 5 cm/1 × 2 inch strips. Put into a bowl. Pour over the marinade and stir to coat. Leave for 1 hour.

Heat a large heavy pan. Do not add any fat. Remove the beef from the marinade and add it to the pan.

Cook briefly to sear the meat all over, then lift it out with a slotted spoon. Set aside. Add the stock and any remaining marinade to the pan and bring to the boil.

Add the celery and carrots to the pan. Boil for 5 minutes, then add the mushrooms, spring onions, Chinese leaves, bean curd and beef. Simmer together for 2 to 3 minutes, then place the pan over a burner and regulate the heat so that the stock simmers slowly whilst the hotpot is eaten.

COCONUT BEEF CURRY

Serves 8

This is one of the driest of Thai curries, and usually quite fiery. Use fewer chillies if you like.

INGREDIENTS

60 ml/2.5 fl oz corn oil

325 g/11 oz beef sirloin, cut into
1¼- x ¾- x ¼-inch pieces

750 ml/25 fl oz thin coconut milk

1 tbsp Thai fish sauce

2 tsp sugar

2 kaffir lime leaves, finely sliced

1 tsp roughly chopped lime peel

2 fresh red chillies, sliced

40 g/1.5 oz basil leaves, for garnish

CURRY PASTE

6 dried red chillies, roughly chopped

7 white peppercorns

4 garlic cloves, roughly chopped

3 shallots, roughly chopped

2 freshly chopped coriander stems

2 tsp salt

1 tsp grated fresh galangal or root
ginger

1 tsp roughly chopped lemongrass

1 tsp prawn paste

Place all the curry paste ingredients in a mortar and pound with a pestle to form a paste. Alternatively, use a spice mill.

Heat the oil in a pan or wok and cook the curry paste for 3 to 4 minutes. Add the beef and stir-fry for 2 minutes, then add the coconut milk and cook over medium heat for about 15 minutes, or until the beef is tender.

Add the fish sauce, sugar, lime leaves and chillies. Transfer to a serving plate and sprinkle with the chopped lime peel and basil.

STIR-FRIED BEEF WITH GARLIC AND CHILLIES

Serves 3 to 4

Garlic and chillies give the character to this simple, tasty stir-fry, but the number of each can be adjusted according to personal taste.

INGREDIENTS

450 g/1 lb sirloin steak, cut into strips

2 tbsp soy sauce

1 spring onion, with the white and green parts thinly sliced

1½ tsp sesame oil

2 tbsp rice wine or dry sherry

1½ tsp sugar

1½ tbsp vegetable oil

3 garlic cloves, cut into slivers

4 fresh red chillies, seeded and cut into strips

Fried Egg-Strip Garnish (see Stir-Fried Chicken, page 82), and toasted sesame seeds

Put the beef strips in a bowl. Add the soy sauce, spring onion, sesame oil, rice wine or dry sherry and sugar. Stir, then set aside to marinate for 1 hour.

Heat the oil in a frying pan. Add the garlic and chillies, and stir-fry for about 1 minute over high heat until fragrant. Remove with a slotted spoon and reserve until later.

Lift the beef out of the marinade, and add the strips to the frying pan. Stir-fry for 2 to 3 minutes. Return the chillies and garlic to the pan. Pour in the marinade and cook, stirring, over medium heat for about 2 minutes. Serve garnished with egg strips and toasted sesame seeds.

PICADILLO

Serves 4 to 6

A Mexican dish that can be made with chopped, ground or thinly sliced beef. It is often used as a filling for tacos or peppers. The most authentic recipes call for chayote, a pear-shaped vegetable belonging to the gourd family. If you cannot get chayote, just leave it out.

INGREDIENTS

900 g/2 lb lean beef

4 tbsp olive oil

1 onion, chopped

2 to 4 garlic cloves, minced

1 chayote, peeled and cubed

1 large potato, peeled and cubed

2 beefsteak tomatoes, cut in chunks

2 carrots, sliced

1 courgette, sliced

3 tbsp raisins

3 or more drained, tinned jalapeño chillies

10 pimiento-stuffed olives, halved

large pinch each of ground cinnamon and cloves

salt and pepper

200 g/7 oz shelled peas, thawed if frozen

50 g/2 oz flaked almonds, for the garnish

Cut the beef in .6 cm/¼ inch wide strips, about 5 cm/2 inches long, or chop finely. Heat 3 tbsp of the oil in a heavy frying pan and sauté the beef strips until browned. Add the onions and garlic and sauté for about 5 minutes, until golden.

Add all the other ingredients, except the peas and almonds. Bring to the boil, then reduce the heat and simmer for 20 to 30 minutes, depending on how well-done you like the vegetables.

About 5 minutes before serving, stir in the peas. When they are tender and the picadillo is thick and flavourful, spoon it into a serving dish and keep very hot.

Heat the remaining olive oil in a small frying pan and fry the almonds until golden. Sprinkle them over the picadillo and serve.

QUICK-COOK BEEF WITH BEAN CURD AND VEGETABLES

Serves 3 to 4

Richness and depth is given to the flavour of this spicy dish by making the stock with miso or *twoenjang*, Korean fermented bean curd. The beef is then cooked for just 2 minutes.

INGREDIENTS

225 g/8 oz sirloin or round steak, cut into
2.5 x 5 cm/1 x 2 inch slices

2 tsp sesame oil

1½ tsp sugar

freshly ground black pepper

8 dried Chinese black mushrooms

1 onion, thinly sliced into rings

1 courgette, sliced

2 spring onions, with the white and green parts sliced

1 to 2 fresh red chilies, seeded and thickly sliced

2 x 100 g/4-oz cakes of medium-firm bean curd, cut into 6 cm/1½-inch chunks

STOCK

8 tbsp miso or *twoenjang* (fermented bean curd)

900 ml/32 fl oz water

2 garlic cloves, lightly crushed

1 onion, cut into chunks

1 carrot, cut into chunks

3 spring onions, with the white and green parts cut into 7.5 cm/3 inch lengths

Make the stock. Put the miso or *twoenjang* in a sieve placed over a saucepan. Slowly pour through the water, pressing the *twoenjang* or miso with the back of a wooden spoon so it is all sieved through. Add the remaining stock ingredients and bring to the boil. Reduce the heat, cover and simmer slowly for 30 minutes.

Meanwhile, place the beef in a bowl and add the sesame oil, sugar and plenty of black pepper. Stir well to coat the slices. Leave for 30 minutes. Soak the Chinese mushrooms in hot water in a separate bowl for the same length of time.

Sieve the stock, squeezing out as much liquid from the vegetables as possible. Pour the stock back into the cleaned pan. Drain the mushrooms and remove the stalks. Add the mushroom caps to the stock with the onion, courgette, spring onions and chillies. Bring to the boil, then reduce the heat and simmer for 2 minutes. Add the beef to the stock with the bean curd. Return to the boil, reduce the heat and simmer for 2 minutes. Serve immediately.

CURRIED MINCED LAMB WITH CAULIFLOWER

Serves 4

INGREDIENTS

3 to 4 whole dried chillies or
1 tsp chilli powder

½ tsp cumin seeds

300 g/10 oz lean minced lamb or beef

1 small onion, chopped

¼ tsp turmeric

½ tsp garam masala

1 tsp salt

200 g/2 oz cauliflower florets

1 tomato, chopped

1 tbsp grated fresh root ginger

3 to 4 fat garlic cloves, minced

2 fresh green chillies, seeded
and sliced

2 to 3 tbsp freshly chopped coriander

coriander sprigs, for the garnish

Heat the oil in a heavy saucepan. Add the dried chillies (do not put the chilli powder in at this stage if you are using it instead) and cumin seeds. Fry these for 30 seconds over medium heat, then add the minced lamb or beef and the onion, stirring continuously.

Add the chilli powder now, if using, then stir in the turmeric, garam masala and salt. Mix thoroughly. Cover the pan, reduce the heat and simmer for 20 to 25 minutes.

Add the cauliflower, tomato, ginger, garlic and the green chillies. Cook over medium heat for 10 to 12 minutes. When the moisture has evaporated, stir in half the coriander. Spoon into a serving dish and sprinkle over the rest of the coriander. Garnish with the coriander sprigs and serve.

SPICY MEATLOAF

Serves 4

This is an excellent party dish because it can be prepared beforehand, chilled a day or two ahead, or frozen and then simply thawed and served cold, or heated on the day.

INGREDIENTS

1 large onion, roughly chopped
2 tsp grated fresh root ginger
2 fresh green chillies, roughly chopped
1 tbsp plain yoghurt
2 to 3 plump garlic cloves
3 tbsp freshly chopped coriander
225 g/8 oz lean minced lamb or beef
1 tbsp cornflour
½ tsp chilli powder
¼ tsp garam masala
small pinch of ground mace
2 tsp lemon juice

cucumber and carrot sticks, onion slices, and lemon slices, for the garnish

Pre-heat the oven to 220°C/425°F/Gas Mark 7. Put the onion, ginger, green chillies, yoghurt, garlic and coriander in a blender and process to a paste.

Put the minced lamb or beef into a bowl and add the paste. Add all the remaining ingredients, except the lemon juice.

Mix the meat thoroughly, kneading it for a couple of minutes to ensure that the herbs and spices are evenly and well distributed.

With moistened hands, press the mixture into a round or oblong loaf shape, making sure that the surface is smooth. Place the loaf in the centre of a piece of aluminium foil large enough to cover it and let it stand for 20 to 30 minutes.

Wrap the loaf and stand it on a baking sheet. Bake for 20 minutes. Unfold the foil to reveal the top of the loaf, then bake it for 5 to 7 minutes more, until it is golden brown. Serve hot or cold, with the garnish.

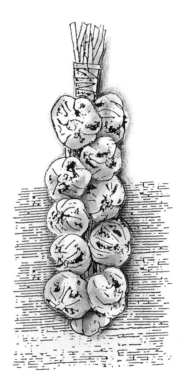

Scorcher Chilli

Serves 4

This chilli is for Texas purists – those who don't hold with beans or tomatoes in their chilli and like it simple and scorching. The beer-based sauce gets its heat from pure *chilli de arbol* powder and unseeded jalapeños, whilst pasilla and mild New Mexico or California pure chilli powders fill out the chilli flavour.

INGREDIENTS

2 tbsp vegetable oil

900 g/2 lb beef, cubed

1 onion, chopped

350 g/12-oz bottle of beer

2 beef stock cubes

3 jalapeño chillies, minced

1 tbsp pure pasilla chilli powder

1 tbsp mild New Mexico or California chilli powder

1 tsp *chilli de arbol* powder

2 tsp ground cumin

2 tsp ground oregano

1 tsp garlic powder

1 tsp ground coriander

2 tbsp masa harina

3 tbsp cold water

about ½ tsp salt

Heat 1 tbsp of the oil in a frying pan and cook the beef until browned. Remove the meat with a slotted spoon. Heat the remaining oil in the cleaned frying pan and sauté the onion for 5 minutes.

Put the beef and sautéed onion in a large pan. Pour in the beer and beef stock and bring to the boil. Add the remaining ingredients, except the masa harina and salt. Reduce the heat and simmer for at least 1½ hours until the meat is tender, adding water if needed.

Mix the masa harina to a paste with the water. Add to the chilli and cook for 2 minutes. Stir in salt to taste, adjust the seasonings and serve.

SIMPLE BEEF AND SALSA CHILLI

Serves 4

This chilli is very easy to make, with bottled salsa providing the heart of the sauce. The spiciness will depend on the type of salsa you use, but can be increased by adding cayenne.

INGREDIENTS

2 tbsp vegetable oil

900 g/2 lb beef, cubed

1 onion, chopped

450 g/1 lb bottled red salsa, preferably chunky

225 g/8-oz can tomato sauce

2 beef stock cubes dissolved in 450 ml/¾ pt hot water

3 tbsp chilli powder

1 tsp ground cumin

1 tsp dried oregano

cayenne pepper to taste

salt, if needed

Heat 1 tbsp of the oil in a frying pan and cook the beef until lightly browned. Remove the meat with a slotted spoon. Heat the remaining oil in the cleaned frying pan and sauté the onion for 5 minutes.

Put the beef, onion, salsa and tomato sauce in a large saucepan. Add the beef stock, then stir in the chilli powder, cumin and oregano. Bring to the boil, reduce the heat and simmer for about 1½ hours or until the meat is tender. Stir occasionally, adding water if needed. Taste, then add cayenne and salt if needed.

BEEF FAJITAS

Serves 4

Fajitas can be made from a poorer-quality cut of beef, in which case the meat is marinated in the sauce for a longer period of time before being sliced across the grain and barbecued over a fierce heat. Fajitas should be served immediately, which is why many restaurants call this dish "sizzling beef". For this recipe, a better quality beef has been used but if you prefer, substitute stewing steak.

INGREDIENTS

275 ml/½ pint dry red wine

1 tbsp Worcestershire sauce

75 ml/3 fl oz sunflower oil

4 red Scotch Bonnet chillies, seeded and sliced

1 tbsp roughly chopped fresh oregano

225 g/8 oz rump steak, trimmed and cut into thin strips

1 red onion, cut into thin wedges

1 small red pepper, seeded and cut into thin strips

1 small yellow pepper, seeded and cut into thin strips

1 courgette, trimmed and cut into thin strips

8 to 12 wheat tortillas, lightly warmed, soured cream, Green Chilli Sauce (page 174) and Guacamole (page 18), to serve

Mix the wine, Worcestershire sauce, 3 tbsp of the oil, half the chillies and the oregano in a bowl. Put the beef into a shallow dish and pour the wine marinade over. Cover and leave for at least 1 hour. Drain, reserving a little of the marinade.

Heat the remaining oil in a wok or large pan and quickly fry the remaining chillies and the vegetables for 3 to 5 minutes, or until crisp and slightly blackened on the edges. Remove from the pan and reserve.

Fry the beef in batches in the remaining pan oil for 2 to 3 minutes, or until sealed and browned. Drain on absorbent kitchen paper. When all the meat has been browned, return the

vegetables and 3 to 4 tbsp of the reserved marinade to the pan and heat through over a fierce heat, stirring frequently.

To serve, spread each warmed tortilla with soured cream, then place some of the beef mixture on top and add a spoonful of the chilli sauce. Roll up and eat with extra green chilli sauce and guacamole.

KITCHEN SINK CHILLI

Serves 12

This moderately spicy chilli has beef, turkey sausage, tomatoes, mushrooms, olives, beans – everything but the kitchen sink.

INGREDIENTS

1.5 kg/3 lb minced beef

450 g/1 lb turkey sausage

450 ml/16 fl oz water

3 onions, chopped

6 garlic cloves, minced

½ green pepper, finely chopped

750 ml/25 fl oz beef stock

225 g/8-oz tin tomato sauce

400 g/14-oz tin chopped tomatoes

60 g/2 oz mild *chilli molido*

1 tbsp hot chilli powder

1 tbsp ground cumin

1 tbsp dried oregano

¼ tsp ground allspice

150 g/6 oz sliced mushrooms

2 × 60 g/2¼-oz tins sliced olives

3 × 450 g/1 lb tins kidney or pinto beans

salt, to taste

Crumble the beef and sausage into a large saucepan. Cook, stirring to break up any large lumps, until browned. Spoon off and discard the fat.

Add all the remaining ingredients, except the olives, beans and salt. Stir well, bring to the boil, then reduce the heat and simmer for 1 hour, stirring occasionally and adding water if needed. Stir in the olives and beans, and simmer for 15 minutes more. Add some salt to taste, adjust the seasonings and serve.

SPICY LIVER SALAD

Serves 4

Liver loses its image as a less-than-exciting variety meat when it gets a flavour boost from chillies and fish sauce.

INGREDIENTS

60 ml/2.5 fl oz chicken stock

325 g/11 oz beef liver, thinly sliced

25 g/1 oz sliced shallots

30 g/1 oz freshly chopped mint leaves

3 spring onions, finely chopped

60 ml/2.5 fl oz lime or lemon juice

2 tbsp sticky rice, dry-fried for a few minutes and pounded finely

2 tbsp crushed dried red chilli

2 tbsp Thai fish sauce

lettuce leaves, for serving

Pour the chicken stock into a frying pan and bring to the boil. Add the liver and cook until medium rare. If you prefer to cook the liver for slightly longer, do so, but do not overcook or the meat will be tough and leathery.

Remove the pan from the heat and drain off all the liquid. Stir in the shallots, chopped mint, spring onions and lime or lemon juice, with the pounded rice, crushed dried chilli and fish sauce. Mix well.

Serve on a bed of lettuce and garnish with the chopped mint leaves.

COOK'S TIP

Beef liver has quite a strong flavour, and is not to everyone's taste, but it is perfect for this spicy dish. You could also use chicken livers for a warm salad on mixed leaves; reduce the amount of crushed chilli if you do, or use hot pepper sauce instead (see page 177).

BREDIE

Serves 6

Bredie is a South African stew made from mutton, tomato juice and dried spotted beans similar to pinto beans. Its exotic combination of seasonings – cardamom, fennel and ginger – often includes some form of chillies. This version, made with lamb shanks, is mildly spicy, but can be made hotter with hot pepper sauce.

INGREDIENTS

2 lamb shanks

2 bay leaves

175 g/6 oz dry pinto beans, picked over and soaked overnight

2 tbsp vegetable oil

1 large onion, chopped

2 garlic cloves, minced

1 tsp fresh root ginger, grated

1 tsp ground coriander

¼ tsp ground cardamom

1 tsp fennel seed

½ tsp dried thyme

1 tsp dried oregano

2 tbsp chilli powder

450 ml/16 fl oz tomato juice

175 g/6-oz tin tomato paste

1 to 2 tsp salt

hot pepper sauce to taste

Put the lamb shanks and bay leaves in a large saucepan and add water to cover. Bring to the boil, reduce the heat and simmer gently for 45 minutes.

Drain the beans and add them to the lamb, then pour in enough water to cover the mixture by 2.5 cm/1 inch. Return to the boil, reduce the heat and simmer for 30 minutes. Remove the lamb shanks and let cool slightly whilst you prepare the other ingredients.

Heat the oil in a large frying pan and sauté the onion and garlic for 2 minutes. Add the ginger, coriander, cardamom, fennel seed, thyme and oregano. Sauté for 5 minutes more. Add to the beans, with the chilli

powder, tomato juice and paste. Return to the boil, reduce the heat and continue simmering, stirring occasionally and adding a little water if needed.

When the lamb has cooled enough to handle, cut the meat from the bones. Discard the fat, then shred the meat and add it to the bean mixture. Cook for 1 to 1¼ hours more, or until the beans are tender. Just before serving, stir in salt and hot pepper sauce to taste.

LAMB IN SPICY YOGHURT SAUCE

Serves 4

INGREDIENTS

2 tbsp sunflower or olive oil

4 lean boneless lamb steaks, about
250 g/5 oz each

I onion, sliced

2 garlic cloves, crushed

3 green New Mexico chillies, peeled,
seeded and sliced

I tsp ground cumin

½ tsp ground cloves

I tsp ground cinnamon

12 green cardamom pods

150 ml/¼ pint water

150 ml/2 oz plain yoghurt

2 tbsp ground almonds

2 tbsp flaked almonds, toasted

flat-leaved parsley, for the garnish

Heat the oil in a frying pan and seal the lamb steaks on both sides. Lift out and drain on absorbent kitchen paper, then set aside.

Add the onion, garlic and chillies to the oil remaining in the pan and sauté for 5 minutes, or until soft. Stir in the spices and cook for 3 minutes more. Stir in the water and bring to the boil. Reduce the heat and add the lamb, then simmer for 10 minutes.

Stir the yoghurt and ground almonds into the pan and cook over low heat for a further 15 minutes, or until the lamb is tender. Stir frequently during this time. If the sauce is thickening too much, add a little extra water.

Transfer the mixture to a heated serving dish, sprinkle with the toasted almonds and garnish with parsley.

KASHMIR LAMB

Serves 4

Kashmir dishes are usually rich and creamy, and often include the cashews that grow so well in this area. They owe their red color to *ratan jot*, a red herb food colouring.

INGREDIENTS

3 tbsp sunflower oil or ghee

1 large onion, sliced

2 garlic cloves

2 or 3 red New Mexico chillies, seeded and sliced

2.5 cm/1 inch piece of fresh root ginger, peeled and grated

1 tsp ground cumin

1 tsp turmeric

1 tsp *ratan jot* or few drops of red food colouring

450 g/1 lb lamb tenderloin, trimmed and cubed

4 tomatoes, peeled, seeded and chopped

450 ml/¾ pt lamb or vegetable stock

25 g/1 oz pistachio nuts

50 g/2 oz cashew nuts

25 g/1 oz sultanas

1 tbsp freshly chopped coriander

freshly cooked rice, to serve

Heat the oil or ghee in a large pan, and sauté the onion, garlic, chillies and ginger for 5 minutes. Add the spices and sauté for 3 minutes more, then stir in the *ratan jot* or food colouring. Add the lamb in two batches and cook for 5 minutes, or until sealed, stirring frequently.

Add the tomatoes and stock, then bring to the boil. Cover, reduce the heat and simmer for 40 minutes.

Stir in the nuts and sultanas. Simmer for 15 minutes more, or until the meat is tender. Stir in the coriander and serve with freshly cooked rice.

NEW MEXICO CHILLI WITH LAMB

Serves 4 to 6

Lamb is a staple of the Navajo Indians of New Mexico and is frequently prepared in stews. Fresh New Mexico green chillies are traditional, but Anaheim or poblano chillies or a combination can be substituted.

INGREDIENTS

2 tbsp vegetable oil

900 g/2 lb lamb, cubed

1½ medium onions, chopped

4 garlic cloves, minced

8 fresh New Mexico, Anaheim or poblano chillies or a combination

225 g/8-oz can tomato sauce

2 to 4 fresh jalapeño or serrano chillies, minced

1 tsp dried oregano

¼ tsp dried sage

50 g/2 oz freshly chopped coriander

about 1 tsp salt

Heat the oil in a large, deep frying pan and cook the lamb until browned on all sides. If the frying pan is large enough, add the onion and garlic and cook for 5 minutes more, then transfer to a large saucepan. If the frying pan is not large enough, first remove the lamb to a large pan, then add additional oil to the frying pan, if needed, and sauté the onion and garlic before adding the mixture to the lamb. Pour in 250 ml water. Bring 8 fl oz to the boil, reduce the heat and simmer for at least 1½ hours.

While the lamb is simmering, roast the green chillies (but not the jalapeños or serranos). Place them in a grill and cook, turning, until all sides are blistered and blackened. Remove the chillies and immediately put them in a plastic bag or bowl (covered with absorbent kitchen paper) to steam for at least 10 minutes. Peel the chillies and remove the stems and seeds.

Chop half the roasted chillies and add them to the stew. Put the rest in a blender or food processor with the tomato sauce and purée until smooth. Add the purée to the stew, along with the jalapeños or serranos, the oregano and sage. Approximately 10 minutes before the chilli is cooked, add the fresh coriander and salt. Taste and adjust the seasonings.

STEWED LAMB WITH HABANEROS

Serves 4 to 6

Beer is the secret ingredient in this spicy dish from the Netherlands Antilles. Use hot pepper sauce instead of minced chillies if you prefer.

INGREDIENTS

2 tbsp vegetable oil

900 g/2 lb boneless lamb, cut into 5 cm/2 inch cubes

2 medium onions, chopped

4 garlic cloves, chopped

50 g/2 oz chopped celery

1 tsp finely chopped fresh root ginger

3 tbsp minced habanero chillies

1 small green pepper, seeded and chopped

2 medium tomatoes, peeled and chopped

1 tbsp lime or lemon juice

1 tsp ground cumin

1 tsp ground allspice

200 ml/⅓ pint beer

1 tbsp red wine vinegar

1 large cucumber, peeled and chopped

60 ml/2.5 fl oz pitted green olives (optional)

1 tbsp capers (optional)

Heat the vegetable oil in a Dutch oven over medium-high heat. Brown the lamb on all sides, then lift out the cubes with a slotted spoon and place them in a bowl. Add the onions, garlic, celery, ginger, chillies and green pepper to the oil remaining in the pan, and sauté until the onions are soft.

Return the lamb cubes to the pan and stir in the tomatoes, lime or lemon juice, cumin and allspice. Cover with beer. Bring to just below the boil, then reduce the heat and simmer for about 1½ hours, until the meat is very tender and starts to fall apart. Add more beer if necessary.

Stir in the vinegar and chopped cucumber, with the olives and capers if using. Simmer for 15 minutes more before serving.

PORK CHILLI WITH SMOKED PAPRIKA

Serves 4

This chilli is only mildly spicy, but the pungent flavour is rounded out by the addition of smoked paprika. Use regular paprika if you cannot locate smoked, but increase the quantity to 1 tablespoon.

INGREDIENTS

1 tbsp vegetable oil

900 g/2 lb pork, cubed

1½ onions, chopped

1 celery stalk, finely chopped

750 ml/25 fl oz chicken stock

225 g/8-oz tin tomato sauce

2 tsp smoked paprika

1 tbsp chilli powder

1 tsp dried oregano

about 1 tsp salt

soured cream, for the topping

Heat the oil in a large, deep frying pan or saucepan and cook the pork until lightly browned on all sides. Add the onion and celery and cook for 5 minutes, stirring frequently.

Add the stock, tomato sauce, paprika, chilli powder and oregano. Bring to the boil, reduce the heat and simmer for 1½ to 2 hours, adding water if needed. Add salt to taste. Serve with a swirl of soured cream on each portion.

SZECHUAN HOT CHILLI PORK

Serves 4

Szechuan cuisine is becoming increasingly popular in the West and there are many different variations on any Szechuan dish. Some err on the sweet side, but nearly all have a strong chilli flavour.

INGREDIENTS

2 tbsp sunflower or groundnut oil

2.5 cm/1 inch piece fresh root ginger, peeled and grated

2 or 3 hontaka or Thai red chillies, seeded and chopped

350 g/12 oz pork tenderloin, trimmed and cut into thin strips

1 red pepper, seeded and cut into strips

1 yellow pepper, seeded and cut into strips

6 spring onions, sliced diagonally

1 tbsp tomato purée mixed with 1 tbsp water

2 tsp soy sauce

1 tsp honey

1 tsp sesame oil

spring onion tassel and flat-leaved parsley, to garnish

Heat the oil in a wok or large pan and stir-fry the ginger and chillies for 2 minutes. Add the pork and stir-fry for a further 4 to 5 minutes. Then add the peppers and cook for 2 minutes. Add the spring onions and stir-fry for 30 seconds. Then add the tomato purée mixture, the soy sauce and honey. Stir-fry for 1 minute, than add the sesame oil and give one more stir. Serve immediately, garnished with a spring onion tassel and the parsley.

COOK'S TIP

A spring onion tassel makes a very effective garnish: simply trim the spring onion to a length of about 15 cm/6 in, then make a series of parallel lengthwise slits in the white part. Place the spring onion in iced water for about 4 hours and the white strips will curl.

◀ Pork Chilli with Smoked Paprika

QUICK JERK PORK CHOPS

Serves 4

In the Caribbean, chillies are called hot peppers, and are often used to make a spice rub for flavouring chicken breasts, lamb, or pork chops or ribs. Marinate the chops overnight if you have time. Next day, all you have to do is throw them on the grill.

INGREDIENTS

25 g/1 oz chopped red chillies

60 g/2 oz fresh allspice berries or 3 tbsp ground allspice

3 tbsp lime juice

2 tbsp chopped green onion

1 tsp Hot, Hot, Hot Pepper Sauce (page 177)

1 tsp ground cinnamon

1 tsp ground nutmeg

4 centre-cut pork chops

cucumber slices and small tomato wedges, for the garnish

In a food processor or blender, purée the chillies, allspice, lime juice, green onion, hot pepper sauce, cinnamon and nutmeg to make a thick paste. Rub the mixture into the chops and arrange them in a single layer in a shallow dish. Cover and marinate in the refrigerator for 1 hour or more.

Grill the chops over a hot charcoal fire or grill in a hot grill until done. The seasonings will cause the chops to char on the outside. Garnish and serve.

SZECHUAN NOODLES WITH PORK AND CHILLIES

Serves 4

Chilli-spiced pork served on a crisp cake of fried noodles is the perfect way to warm up on a cold winter's night.

INGREDIENTS

350 g/12 oz Chinese egg noodles

1 tbsp cornflour

3 tbsp dry sherry

90 ml/3.5 fl oz chicken stock

90 ml/3.5 fl oz light soy sauce

90 ml/3.5 fl oz oil

2 fresh green chillies, seeded and chopped

2 garlic cloves, crushed

5 cm/2 inch piece fresh root ginger, peeled, and cut into fine strips

225 g/8 oz lean boneless pork, cut into fine strips

1 red pepper, seeded, and cut into fine, short strips

1 bunch green onions, cut diagonally into fine slices

200 g/7-oz can bamboo shoots, drained and cut in strips

2.5 cm/1 inch slice Chinese cabbage head, separated into pieces

Place the noodles in a pan and pour in enough boiling water to cover them. Bring back to the boil and cook for 2 minutes. While the noodles are cooking, mix the cornflour with the sherry, stock and soy sauce, then set aside. Drain the noodles.

Wipe the pan and heat the oil. Add the noodles, spreading them out thinly and fry over medium to high heat until they are crisp and golden underneath, patting them down slightly into a thin cake – they will set more or less in shape. Use a large spatula to turn the noodle cake over and brown the second side. Don't worry if the noodles break up slightly – the aim is to end up with some that are crisp, and others that remain soft. Transfer the noodles to a large serving dish and keep hot.

Add the chillies, garlic, ginger and pork strips to the oil remaining in the pan. Stir-fry the mixture over high heat until the pork is browned. Add the red pepper and green onions and stir-fry for 2 minutes more, then add the bamboo shoots. Stir-fry for 1 minute to heat the bamboo shoots.

Give the cornflour mixture a stir and pour it into the pan. Bring to the boil, stirring, and cook over high heat for 30 seconds. Mix in the Chinese cabbage and stir for just long enough to heat it. Spoon the pork mixture over the noodles and serve at once.

FEIJOADA

Serves 8 to 10

Feijoada, a spicy stew of black beans and pork, is the ceremonial dish of Brazil. Traditionally it is made with various parts of the pig, such as the snout, ears, tail and feet. This hot Americanized version uses pork loin and linguica, a garlicky Portuguese sausage. Serve Feijoada with rice, greens and orange slices.
If you cannot find *chillies de arbol,* any small hot dried red chillies will do.

INGREDIENTS

400 g/14 oz dry black beans, picked over and soaked overnight

4 tbsp vegetable oil

3 whole dried *chillies de arbol*

8 garlic cloves, minced

900 g/2 lb pork loin, cubed

1 large onion, chopped

400 g/14-ounce tin chopped tomatoes

450 g/1 lb linguica, cut into .6 cm/¼ inch slices

3 jalapeño chillies, minced

about 2 tsp salt

orange twists, for the garnish

boiled rice, for serving

Drain the beans, put them in a heavy saucepan and add enough water to cover by 5 cm/2 in. Bring to the boil, reduce the heat and simmer.

Heat 1 tablespoon of the oil in a small frying pan and sauté the *chillies de arbol* and half the minced garlic for 1 to 2 minutes, until the garlic just starts to brown. Add to the beans.

Heat another tablespoon of oil in a large frying pan and cook the pork until lightly browned. Lift out the pork with a slotted spoon and add it to the black beans.

Heat the remaining oil in a frying pan and sauté the onion with the remaining garlic for 5 minutes, then add to the beans.

Add the tomatoes and linguica to the beans. Return the stew to the boil, reduce the heat and simmer for 1 hour. Stir in the jalapeños and continue to simmer the stew for 30 minutes to 1 hour, until the beans are tender. Add the salt, taste the stew and adjust the seasonings. Garnish with orange twists and serve with rice.

PORK AND CHILLI BALLS

Serves 4

INGREDIENTS

450 g/1 lb lean minced pork

3 lemongrass stalks, outer leaves discarded, minced

1 tsp Red Chilli Paste (page 174)

grated zest of 1 lime

3 tomatoes, peeled, seeded and finely chopped

1 tsp turmeric

2 tsp minced, fresh gingerroot

1 garlic clove, minced

¼ tsp salt

oil for deep-frying

lime wedges, whole star anise, coriander sprigs, and chilli flowers, for the garnish

boiled rice, for serving

Put the pork, lemongrass, chilli paste and lime zest into a bowl. Stir in the tomatoes, turmeric, ginger, garlic and salt. Mix well.

Using slightly wet hands, form the pork mixture into small balls, each about the size of an apricot. Place on a tray, cover and chill for 30 minutes.

Heat the oil for deep-frying to 180°C/350°F/Gas Mark 4. Fry the pork balls in batches for 5 to 6 minutes, or until golden. Remove with a slotted spoon and drain on absorbent kitchen paper. Serve hot on a bed of rice, garnished with lime wedges, whole star anise, coriander sprigs and chilli flowers.

BRAISED GAMMON WITH CHILLI SAUCE

Serves 4

INGREDIENTS

3 fresh red poblano chillies

1 garlic clove

4 tbsp olive or sunflower oil

2 tbsp orange juice

2 tsp honey, warmed

4 gammon steaks, trimmed of excess fat

2 tbsp butter

180 ml/6.5 fl oz dry white wine

180 ml/6.5 fl oz chicken or vegetable stock

7.5 cm/3 inch piece of cucumber, peeled and cut into julienne strips

1 tbsp cornflour mixed with 1 tbsp water

orange wedges and fresh herbs, for the garnish

Pre-heat the grill. Place the chillies in the grill pan and grill for 10 minutes, or until the skins have blistered and charred. Put into a plastic bag for 10 minutes to soften, then peel and remove the seeds.

Chop the chillies roughly and put them in a food processor. Add the garlic, oil, orange juice, and honey. Process until smooth, then brush the marinade over both sides of the gammon steaks. Leave in a cool place for at least 30 minutes.

Melt the butter in a large frying pan and seal the steaks quickly on both sides. Add any remaining chilli marinade and pour in the wine and stock. Bring to the boil, then reduce the heat and simmer for 5 to 8 minutes, or until the steaks are cooked. Drain and place on warmed serving plates.

Add the cucumber to the pan and stir in the cornflour mixture. Cook, stirring occasionally, for 2 minutes, or until the sauce has thickened. Pour over the steaks, and garnish with the orange wedges and fresh herbs.

VEGETARIAN CHOICE

SPICY VEGETABLE CRUNCH

Serves 4

INGREDIENTS

3 tbsp oil

3 to 4 whole dried chillies

1 tsp cumin seeds

¼ tsp turmeric

½ tsp salt

100 g/4 oz cauliflower florets

cut green beans

½ red pepper, seeded and diced

½ green pepper, seeded and diced

135 g/5 oz diced carrots

2 tomatoes, chopped

2 tsp grated fresh root ginger

3 to 4 plump garlic cloves, minced

1 fresh green chilli, chopped

2 to 3 tbsp freshly chopped coriander

Heat the oil in a large frying pan. Break the dried chillies into the frying pan and add the cumin seeds. When both begin to sizzle, add the turmeric and salt. Stir, then add all the vegetables, including the tomato. Stir-fry for 2 minutes.

Add the ginger, garlic and green chillies, and stir to mix thoroughly.

Lower the heat, cover the pan tightly, and steam cook the vegetables for 12 to 15 minutes until crisp-tender. Sprinkle with the coriander and serve.

BLACK-EYED PEAS IN GINGER SAUCE

Serves 4

Vegetarian dishes can be accused of being a bit bland. Not this one – the combination of root ginger and chilli gives black-eyed peas a marvellous flavour.

INGREDIENTS

200 g/7 oz dried black-eyed peas, picked over and soaked overnight

875 ml/1⅓ pints water

2 tsp grated fresh root ginger

½ tsp chilli powder

¼ tsp turmeric

½ tsp salt

1 to 2 fresh green chillies, seeded

1 tbsp plain yoghurt

1 tbsp oil

1 large onion, sliced

½ tsp cumin seeds

4 to 5 garlic cloves, chopped

¼ tsp Garam Masala

2 to 3 tbsp freshly chopped coriander

Drain the black-eyed peas and place them in a heavy pan. Add the water and bring to the boil. Stir in half the ginger, the chilli powder, turmeric and salt, then reduce the heat, cover the pan and cook slowly for 45 to 50 minutes.

Add the remaining ginger, the green chillies, and the yoghurt. Mix well and let the mixture simmer for another 10 to 15 minutes, or until the beans are tender.

Heat the oil in a small frying pan and sauté the onion for 3 to 4 minutes over medium heat. When it is starting to colour, add the cumin seeds and chopped garlic. Remove the pan from the heat just as the garlic is turning golden brown.

Pour the mixture into the simmering peas, then stir in the garam masala. Cook for 5 minutes, then stir in the coriander and serve.

COOK'S TIP
Use tamarind pulp instead of yoghurt if you can locate any. If you use the instant concentrated tamarind, you will only need to add 1 tsp.

CAULIFLOWER AND TOMATO CURRY

Serves 4

If dried chillies are not available, use 3 or 4 green fresno chillies or 1 to 1½ tsp medium-hot chilli powder.

INGREDIENTS

5 dried ancho chillies

300 g/3 oz cauliflower florets

150 g/6 oz diced potatoes

2 tbsp sunflower oil

5 cm piece of root ginger, peeled and sliced

1 onion, sliced

2 garlic cloves, minced

1 tsp coriander seeds

1 tsp cumin seeds

1 tsp fenugreek seeds

1 tsp turmeric

2 tbsp tomato purée mixed with 2 tbsp water

300 g/3 oz peeled, seeded and chopped tomatoes

180 ml/6.5 fl oz coconut milk

75 g/3 oz plain yoghurt, plus extra for the garnish

fresh flat-leaved parsley or coriander, to garnish

poppadoms or naan bread, for serving

Roast the dried chillies in a non-stick frying pan for 2 to 3 minutes, taking care not to let them scorch. Tip into a bowl and add hot (not boiling) water. Soak for at least 10 minutes until soft, then chop the chillies and set them aside.

Bring a saucepan of lightly salted water to the boil. Add the cauliflower florets and cook for 3 minutes, then lift out with a slotted spoon. Add the potatoes to the pan and boil for 10 minutes. Drain and reserve.

Heat the oil in the cleaned pan and gently sauté the ginger for 3 minutes, then lift out and discard the ginger. Add the onion, garlic, and chopped re-hydrated chillies to the flavoured oil and sauté for 3 minutes. Stir in the spices and cook, stirring frequently, for 3 minutes.

Add the tomato purée mixture to the pan with the tomatoes and coconut milk. Bring to just below boiling point and cook for 5 minutes. Add the reserved cauliflower and potatoes, and cook for 5 to 8 minutes longer, or until the vegetables are just tender.

Stir in the yoghurt and heat through gently for 2 minutes. Drizzle the extra yoghurt over when serving and garnish with fresh parsley or coriander. Serve with poppadoms or naan bread.

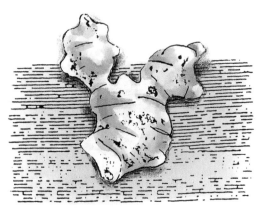

CHEESE-FILLED CHILLIES IN BATTER JACKETS

Serves 4

You need large chillies for this Mexican recipe: Anaheims or poblanos are best. Stuffing them takes time, but the taste is sensational and well worth the effort. Tinned chillies won't give quite such good results, but are worth using if you are in a hurry.

INGREDIENTS

12 fresh Anaheim or poblano chillies

450 g/1 lb finely grated Cheddar or Monterey Jack cheese

115 g/4 oz plain flour

6 eggs, separated

oil for deep-frying

boiled rice and refried beans, for serving

Pre-heat the grill. Place the chillies in the grill pan and grill until the skins blister and start to blacken. Place in a strong plastic bag – or in a bowl, covered with absorbent kitchen paper – and leave for 10 minutes.

Slit the side of each chilli carefully and remove the seeds and veins, taking care not to break the flesh. Shape a small amount of grated cheese to fit the chilli, tapering it as needed, and ease into place. Stuff the remaining chillies in the same way.

Spread out the flour in a shallow bowl. Beat the egg yolks in a second bowl until pale and thick. In a bowl, whisk the egg whites until stiff, then fold them into the yolks to make a simple batter. Heat the oil for deep-frying. Working quickly, roll each filled chilli in flour, then dip it in the batter, making sure that the entire surface is coated. Deep-fry the coated chillies in batches, until the batter coating is crisp and golden, then drain on absorbent kitchen paper. Keep hot while cooking successive batches. Serve immediately, with rice and refried beans.

CHILLI WITH PEACHES AND THREE BEANS

Serves 12

This vegetarian chilli is so delicious, everyone will want some. Serve it on its own, with rice or noodles, or as a filling for baked potatoes.

INGREDIENTS

1 red pepper, roughly chopped
2 green peppers, roughly chopped
1 large onion, roughly chopped
2 peaches, peeled, and roughly chopped
800 g/28-oz tinned tomatoes, coarsely chopped
800 g/28-oz tin tomato sauce
1 tsp hot pepper sauce
¼ tsp dried thyme
1 tsp dried oregano
2 tsp ground cumin, or more to taste
1 tbsp chilli powder
1 tsp ground black pepper
225 ml/8 fl oz water
825 g/19-oz tin cannellini beans
2 x 450 g/1 lb cans black beans
450 g/1 lb tin kidney beans
salt (optional)

Put all the ingredients, except the beans, in a heavy saucepan and stir well. Bring to the boil, reduce the heat and simmer for 30 minutes, stirring often to keep the chilli from scorching, and adding more water if needed.

Add the beans, with enough liquid for the desired consistency. Simmer for 15 minutes more. Taste and add salt, if needed.

OKRA AND BEAN CURRY

Serves 4

It is possible to make a delicious vegetable curry in under half an hour, as this simple recipe proves.

INGREDIENTS

2 tbsp sunflower oil

I large onion, sliced

2 garlic cloves, crushed

4 fresh Kenyan or green fresno chillies, seeded and sliced

I tsp ground coriander

I tsp ground cumin

5 cloves, ground

8 green cardamom pods

I tsp turmeric

I tsp fenugreek seeds, lightly bruised

450 ml/16 fl oz vegetable stock

450 g/1 lb okra, trimmed

drained tinned pinto or kidney beans, rinsed

60 ml/2 oz plain yoghurt

2 tbsp freshly chopped coriander

2 tbsp flaked almonds, toasted

Heat the oil in a pan and sauté the onion, garlic and chillies for 5 minutes. Add the spices and sauté for 3 minutes more. Stir in the stock and bring to the boil. Cover the pan, reduce the heat and simmer for 10 minutes more.

Prick the okra a few times with a fork and add to the pan with the beans. Cook gently for 8 to 10 minutes, or until the okra is tender.

Stir in the yoghurt and coriander, and heat through briefly, without boiling. Serve sprinkled with the almonds.

SPINACH AND POTATO SAMOSAS

Serves 4

Folding filo pastry to make samosas is fun and it doesn't take long to master the technique.

INGREDIENTS

3 tbsp sunflower oil

I onion, chopped

3 fresh green fresno chillies, seeded and chopped

I tsp ground cumin

I tsp ground coriander

75 g/3 oz diced potatoes, cooked and well drained

225 g/8 oz chopped spinach, cooked and well drained

4 large sheets of filo pastry, thawed if frozen

oil for deep-frying

Heat the oil in a frying pan and sauté the onion and chillies for 3 minutes, then stir in the spices and cook for 3 minutes more. Stir in the cooked vegetables and mix well. Let cool. Cut the filo into 10 × 10 cm/10 × 4 inch strips. Place 2 tablespoons of the vegetable filling at one end of each strip and fold the dough over diagonally to enclose the filling and form a triangle. Fold the triangle over on itself. Continue along the strip until you have a neat triangular pastry, sealing the final turn with a little water. Heat the oil for deep-frying to 180°C/ 350°F/Gas Mark 4 and fry the samosas in batches for about 5 minutes, until golden. Drain on absorbent kitchen paper and serve with chutney or salsa. A mixed leaf salad would be the ideal accompaniment.

LENTIL AND VEGETABLE CHILLI

Serves 4 to 6

A combination of kidney beans, lentils, peas and carrots makes a chunky vegetarian chilli that can be as mild or as fiery as you choose.

INGREDIENTS

dry kidney beans, picked over and soaked overnight

1 bay leaf

1 tbsp vegetable oil

1 celery stalk, chopped

1 onion, chopped

1 garlic clove, minced

2 tsp chilli powder

½ tsp dried oregano

½ tsp dried basil

400 g/14-oz tin chopped tomatoes

red lentils

100 g/3½ oz sliced carrots

shelled peas, thawed if frozen

salt

cooked peas and carrots, for serving

Drain the beans, put them in a large saucepan and pour in water to cover. Add the bay leaf. Bring to the boil and boil hard for 10 minutes, then reduce the heat and simmer whilst you prepare the remaining ingredients.

Heat the oil in a frying pan and sauté the celery and onion for 5 minutes. Add the garlic and sauté for 5 minutes. Add the contents of the frying pan to the beans, with the chilli powder, oregano, basil and tomatoes. Return to the boil, reduce the heat and simmer for 1 hour, adding water if the mixture becomes too thick.

Stir in the lentils and cook for 10 minutes. Add water if necessary, then add the carrots and cook for 5 minutes more. Stir in the peas and cook for 10 minutes, by which time the lentils should have cooked down to a purée and the beans should be tender. Add salt to taste. Serve with peas and carrots.

SPICED VEGETABLES WITH BEAN CURD

Serves 6

Bean curd has little taste of its own, but readily absorbs the flavour of the spicy sauce to make a valuable contribution to this vegetarian dish. Use smoked bean curd if you prefer.

INGREDIENTS

6 dried ancho, pasilla or New Mexico chillies, or a combination

225 ml/8 fl oz hot water

about 4 tbsp vegetable oil

1 large onion, chopped

1 green pepper, seeded and chopped

2 celery stalks, chopped

4 garlic cloves, minced

450 ml/16 fl oz vegetable stock

225 ml/16 fl oz tomato sauce

400 g/14-oz tin chopped tomatoes

1 tsp ground cumin

1 tsp ground coriander

1 tsp paprika

2 tsp dried oregano

350 g/12 oz firm bean curd or tofu

1 tsp salt

30 g/1 oz freshly chopped coriander

Split the dried chillies in half and remove the stems and seeds. Put the pieces in a small bowl and pour over the hot but not boiling water. Let them steep in the water for 30 minutes, stirring occasionally to be sure all parts of the chillies remain covered with water.

Meanwhile, heat 2 tablespoons of the oil in a large frying pan. Sauté the onion, pepper, celery and garlic for 5 minutes. Put the sautéed vegetables in a large pan and add the stock, tomato sauce, tomatoes, spices and oregano. Stir in the salt. Bring to the boil, reduce the heat and simmer while you make the chilli sauce.

Pour the chillies, with their soaking liquid, into a blender or food processor. Purée until a smooth sauce is formed. Strain the sauce and add it to the simmering vegetable mixture.

Cut the bean curd into .6 cm/¼-inch cubes. Heat the remaining oil in a frying pan and fry the bean curd over medium to high heat for 2 to 3 minutes each side, until the cubes are slightly browned. Add the bean curd to the chilli and simmer for 30 minutes more. Stir in the coriander and salt to taste. Adjust the seasonings if necessary and serve.

COOK'S TIP

If not using firm bean curd, it should be pressed to remove excess water. Place the bean curd on a plate, put another plate on top and weight it with heavy objects. Bean curd should be pressed for at least 30 minutes before frying.

SEASONAL VEGETABLES IN GREEN MASALA

Serves 4

This is a very good tempered recipe; you can vary the vegetables as long as you keep the proportions the same.

INGREDIENTS

2 tbsp oil

3 or 4 whole dried chillies

1 tsp cumin seeds

200 g/8 oz cauliflower florets

135 g/5 oz cut green beans

75 g/3 oz diced carrots

½ red pepper, seeded and diced

½ green pepper, seeded and diced

1 beefsteak tomato, chopped

¼ tsp turmeric

½ to ¾ tsp salt

GREEN MASALA

2 tsp grated fresh root ginger

4 fat garlic cloves, chopped

2 fresh green chillies, chopped

3 tbsp freshly chopped coriander

Heat the oil in a heavy saucepan. Crumble the whole, dried chillies into the pan and add the cumin seeds. Fry for 1 minute, then add all the vegetables, with the turmeric, and salt. Cook for 1 to 2 minutes more, whilst stirring the vegetables together.

Add all the ingredients for the green masala. Stir continuously until the ingredients are well mixed. Cover the pan and simmer over a medium heat for 15 minutes, until the vegetables are crisp-tender. Serve immediately whilst hot.

POTATO CURRY

Serves 4

What could be simpler or more satisfying than this tasty curry?

INGREDIENTS

1 tsp cumin seeds

1 tsp whole coriander seeds

1 tsp fenugreek seeds

5 cloves

6 cardamom pods

2 tbsp sunflower oil

1 large onion, sliced

2 garlic cloves, crushed

4 fresh red jalapeño chillies, seeded and chopped

450 g/1 lb cubed potatoes

600 ml/1 pint vegetable stock

1 red pepper, seeded and sliced

2 tbsp freshly chopped coriander

Grind the whole spices in a spice mill or use a mortar and pestle. Heat the oil in a large pan and sauté the onion, garlic and chillies for 5 minutes, or until softened. Add the ground spices and cook gently for 3 minutes more, stirring occasionally.

Add the potatoes with the stock and bring to the boil. Cover the pan, reduce the heat and simmer for 15 minutes, or until the potatoes are just tender.

Add the sliced red pepper and cook for 5 minutes more. Stir in the freshly chopped coriander and serve.

◀ *Seasonal Vegetables in Green Masala*

MIXED MASALA BEANS

Serves 4 to 6

Not only do the ingredients blend so well together, they also make a very colourful dish.

INGREDIENTS

1 tbsp oil

½ onion, chopped

½ tsp cumin seeds

½ tsp chilli powder

¼ tsp turmeric

¼ tsp garam masala

275 ml/½ pint water

425 g/15-oz tin chick-peas, drained

425 g/15-oz tin kidney beans, drained

1 tomato, chopped

1 or 2 fresh green chillies, chopped

4 garlic cloves

1 tsp grated fresh root ginger

1 green pepper, seeded and chopped

2 tsp lemon juice

2 to 3 tbsp freshly chopped coriander

Heat the oil in a heavy saucepan. Stir in the onion with the cumin seeds and sauté until the onions are pale gold in colour.

Stir in the chilli powder, turmeric, and garam masala. Add 2 tablespoons of the water and cook, stirring continuously for 1 to 2 minutes.

Gently stir in the chick-peas, kidney beans, tomato, green chillies, garlic and ginger. Mix well and stir in the remaining water. Bring to the boil, then reduce the heat and simmer for 15 to 20 minutes.

Add the green pepper and cook for 2 to 3 minutes more. Stir in the lemon juice and half the coriander. Tip into a heated serving dish, sprinkle with the remaining coriander and serve whilst hot.

PASTA WITH SPICY TOMATO SAUCE

Serves 4

INGREDIENTS

2 tbsp olive oil

1 large onion, chopped

1 small fennel bulb, trimmed and chopped

2 garlic cloves, crushed

4 red de agua chillies, seeded and sliced

8 sun-dried tomatoes

450–525 ml/16–19 fl oz vegetable stock

150 g/6 oz grated carrot

150 g/6 oz wiped and sliced oyster mushrooms

2 tbsp tomato purée mixed with 4 tbsp water

1 tsp sugar

salt and pepper

2 red peppers, seeded, blanched and cut into small strips

2 tbsp freshly chopped basil

10 to 12 oz fresh pasta, such as tagliatelle or rigatoni

freshly chopped basil, for the garnish

shaved or freshly grated Parmesan cheese, for serving

Heat the oil in a pan and gently sauté the onion, fennel, garlic, chillies, and sun-dried tomatoes for 3 minutes. Add 180 ml/6.5 fl oz of the stock and simmer for 5 to 8 minutes.

Put into a food processor and process to a chunky purée, adding extra stock if necessary. Return to the pan with the remaining stock.

Add the carrot, mushrooms, tomato purée mixture, sugar and seasoning to taste. Bring to the boil, then reduce the heat and simmer gently for 15 to 20 minutes, or until the sauce is thick. Add the peppers and chopped basil, and cook for 3 to 4 minutes more.

Meanwhile, cook the pasta in boiling salted water for 4 to 6 minutes, or until it rises to the surface of the water and is just tender. Drain and return to the cleaned pan.

Pour over the tomato sauce and toss well over the heat for 2 to 3 minutes. Garnish with the basil, and serve sprinkled with Parmesan cheese.

FRIED THAI NOODLES WITH CHILLIES

Serves 4

Lemongrass and ginger perfume this superb dish from Thailand.

INGREDIENTS

175 g/6 oz instant dried noodles

2 tbsp sunflower oil

2 lemongrass stalks, outer leaves removed, finely chopped

2.5 cm/1 inch piece of root ginger, peeled and grated

1 red onion, cut into thin wedges

2 garlic cloves, crushed

4 red Thai chillies, seeded and sliced

1 red pepper, seeded and cut into matchsticks

1 small carrot, pared with a vegetable peeler into ribbons

1 small courgette, pared with a vegetable peeler into ribbons

100 g/4 oz mange tout, trimmed and cut diagonally in half

6 spring onions, trimmed and diagonally sliced

1 cup cashew nuts

2 tbsp soy sauce

juice of 1 orange

1 tsp honey

1 tbsp sesame oil

Cook the noodles in a saucepan of lightly salted boiling water for 3 minutes. Drain, plunge into cold water, then drain again and reserve.

Heat the oil in a wok or large pan and stir-fry the lemongrass and root ginger for 2 minutes. Using a slotted spoon lift out and discard the lemongrass and root ginger.

Add the onion, garlic and chillies to the oil remaining in the wok or pan and stir-fry for 2 minutes. Add the red pepper and cook for 2 minutes more, then add the remaining vegetables and stir-fry for 2 minutes.

Add the reserved noodles with the cashew nuts, soy sauce, orange juice and honey. Toss over the heat for 1 minute. Drizzle over the sesame oil and cook for 30 seconds. Serve immediately whilst hot.

SPICY BROWN RICE

Serves 4

INGREDIENTS

2 tbsp oil

2 garlic cloves, crushed

1 onion, finely chopped

½ small red pepper, seeded and thinly sliced

2 Anaheim chillies, seeded and chopped

1175 g/6 oz brown rice

750 ml/25 fl oz vegetable stock

salt and pepper

Heat the oil in a large frying pan and sauté the garlic, onion, red pepper and chillies for 5 to 7 minutes, or until the onion is transparent and beginning to brown.

Add the rice and cook for several minutes, stirring constantly.

Pour in the vegetable stock, cover the pan tightly, and cook over a low heat for 30 to 35 minutes, or until the rice is just tender. Season with salt and pepper and serve.

▶ *Fried Thai Noodles with Chillies*

CELLOPHANE NOODLES WITH VEGETABLES

Serves 4

Contrasting textures are a feature of this colourful noodle dish. After the vegetables have been prepared,
it takes very little time to cook.

INGREDIENTS

6 dried Chinese black mushrooms,
soaked in hot water for 30 minutes

150 g/5 oz young fresh spinach leaves

2 Chinese cabbage leaves

3 shiitake or oyster mushrooms, thinly
sliced

4 spring onions, with the white and
green parts thickly sliced diagonally

1 small courgette, cut into fine strips

1 carrot, cut into fine strips

4 tbsp vegetable oil

1 tbsp sesame oil

3 garlic cloves, minced

2 small fresh red chillies, seeded and
cut into fine strips

50 g/2 oz cellophane noodles, soaked
in hot water for 30 minutes and
drained

1 tbsp soy sauce

1 tsp sugar

salt

Drain the dried mushrooms, then cut out and discard the stems and any hard parts. Thinly slice the mushroom caps.

Bring a large saucepan of water to the boil. Add the spinach, cover, and quickly return to the boil. Boil for 2 minutes, then drain and rinse under cold running water and drain again, squeezing out as much water as possible. Separate the leaves and tear any large ones in half.

Cut away and discard the curly outer part of the Chinese cabbage leaves, saving only the 'V'-shaped core of the leaves. Cut this into fine strips, then place in a bowl with the spinach, dried and fresh mushrooms, spring onions, courgette and carrot. Mix well.

Heat the vegetable and sesame oils in a deep frying pan. Add the garlic and chillies and stir-fry for 10 seconds. Add the spinach mixture and stir-fry for 3 to 4 minutes until the vegetables are crisp-tender. Switch the heat to low and stir in the noodles, soy sauce, sugar and salt. Toss over the heat for 2 minutes, then serve.

CHILLI-RICE BURGERS

Serves 6

These burgers can be grilled on the barbecue, but it is a good idea to put them in a basket grill
so that they can be turned over easily.

INGREDIENTS

2 tbsp sunflower oil

2 garlic cloves, minced

4 red de agua chillies, seeded and
chopped

heaping 150 g/5.25 oz short-grain rice

1 large carrot, grated

2 tbsp tomato purée mixed with
2 tbsp water

600 ml/1 pint vegetable stock

salt and pepper

100 g/4 oz drained tinned red kidney
beans

50 g/2 oz sweetcorn kernels

2 tbsp freshly chopped coriander

2 tsp olive oil

1 large tomato, sliced

6 burger baps, lightly toasted

Chilli Pepper Relish (page 28),
for serving

Heat the sunflower oil in a frying pan and sauté the garlic and chillies for 5 minutes. Stir in the rice and continue to cook for 3 minutes, stirring occasionally. Stir in the carrot.

Stir the tomato purée mixture into the pan with the stock. Add seasoning and bring to the boil. Reduce the heat and simmer for 20 minutes, or until the rice is cooked, stirring occasionally and adding a little extra stock if the rice is very dry.

Add the kidney beans and sweetcorn kernels. Cook for 5 minutes more or until the mixture is very stiff and will stick together. Stir in the chopped coriander and remove from the heat. Let cool.

When the mixture is cool enough to handle, wet your hands slightly and shape into six large burgers. Cover and chill for at least 30 minutes.

Preheat the grill to medium. Place the burgers on the grill and brush lightly with a little olive oil. Grill for 4 to 5 minutes, or until heated through, carefully turning the burgers over once during cooking.

Place a slice of tomato on the bottom of each bap and top with a rice burger. Spoon a little relish over, cover with the bap tops and serve with extra relish.

CHEESE TURNOVERS WITH GREEN TOMATO SAUCE

Serves 4

Use bought tortillas to make these turnovers, or prepare your own, following the directions on page 24.

INGREDIENTS

225 g/8 oz grated Cheddar cheese

6 spring onions, trimmed and chopped

30 g/1½ oz pine nuts, toasted

6 dried chipotle chillies, roasted and soaked in hot water for 10 minutes

2 tbsp butter

300 g/12 oz sliced mushrooms

8 prepared wheat tortillas

1 egg, beaten

oil for deep-frying

salad leaves, to serve

SAUCE

150 g/6 oz peeled, seeded and chopped green tomatoes

3 shallots, finely chopped

2 or 3 garlic cloves, crushed

3 fresh green jalapeño chillies, seeded and chopped

180 ml/6.5 fl oz vegetable stock

1 tsp honey

2 tsp arrowroot mixed with 1 tbsp water

2 tbsp freshly chopped flat-leaved parsley

Make the sauce. Put the green tomatoes, shallots, garlic and chillies into a saucepan and simmer for 5 to 7 minutes, or until softened. Tip into a food processor and add the stock and honey. Process to a purée. Sieve into the cleaned pan.

Return the sauce to the pan and simmer for 5 minutes. Stir in the arrowroot mixture and cook, stirring constantly until the sauce thickens and then clears.

Mix the cheese, spring onions and pine nuts in a bowl. Discard the seeds from the re-hydrated chillies and chop the flesh. Add to the cheese mixture and mix well. Set aside.

Melt the butter in a small pan and sauté the mushrooms for 3 minutes. Drain. Place a spoonful of the cheese mixture on top of each tortilla and top with a spoonful of the mushrooms. Brush the edges of each tortilla with a little beaten egg, then fold over to form a crescent shape. Pinch the edges together firmly. Brush the edges lightly with the beaten egg and fold the edges over again to give a rope effect and a more secure seal.

Heat the oil to 180°C/350°F/Gas Mark 4 and fry the turnovers in batches for 2 to 3 minutes, or until golden. Drain on absorbent kitchen paper and serve on a bed of salad leaves. Serve the green sauce separately.

MUSHROOM MASALA OMELETTE

Serves 2

Choose a frying pan which can safely be placed in the grill for making this omelette. The mixture is first fried, then finished in a hot grill.

INGREDIENTS

3 eggs, separated
1 tsp plain flour
25 g/1 oz green or red pepper
37 g/1½ oz chopped mushrooms
1 fresh green chilli, finely chopped
50 g/2 oz thinly sliced onion
½ tsp chilli powder
¼ tsp garlic powder
1 to 2 tbsp freshly chopped coriander
¼ tsp cumin seeds
¼ tsp salt
2 tbsp water
1 tbsp oil

Pre-heat the grill. Grease a large, non-stick frying pan with the oil and heat it to smoking point. Pour in the egg and vegetable mixture, reduce the heat and cook for 1 to 2 minutes, shaking the pan. Then slide the pan under the grill to finish the omelette.

Whisk the egg yolks in a bowl, then fold in the flour and mix well. Add the chopped pepper, mushrooms, green chilli, onion slices and all the spices and herbs. Season with salt.

Whisk the egg whites in a grease-free bowl. Fold into the egg yolk mixture and whisk once again, gradually adding the water.

FRIED EGGS IN A SPICED VEGETABLE NEST

Serves 2

A simple dish which is often cooked for brunch in Indian households.

INGREDIENTS

1 tbsp butter
½ onion, thinly sliced
2 fresh green chillies, chopped
red pepper matchsticks
2 garlic cloves, crushed
pinch of chilli powder
pinch of salt
2 tbsp water
2 eggs
freshly ground black pepper
2 tbsp snipped chives

Melt the butter in a non-stick frying pan and cook the onion and green chillies over low heat for 4 to 5 minutes, adding a tiny amount of water between stirs to keep them from sticking and burning.

Add the pepper and garlic and cook for 3 to 4 minutes, stirring continuously. Stir in the chilli powder, salt and water and simmer again for 2 to 3 minutes.

Break the eggs gently on top of the bed of spiced vegetables in the pan, taking care to keep the egg yolks intact. Shake the pan so that the egg white spreads to fill the pan. Do not overcook the egg yolks – they are done when, if you were to pierce them with a fork, they would ooze out and run slightly.

Grind black pepper over the surface, sprinkle with chives and serve immediately.

COURGETTE AND CHILLI PANCAKES

Serves 4

These tasty little pancakes are ideal for serving with a vegetable stir-fry.

INGREDIENTS

shredded courgette

1 or 2 fresh green chillies, seeded and sliced

1 tbsp minced garlic

2 spring onions, finely chopped

salt and pepper

1 egg, lightly beaten

3 tbsp plain flour

vegetable oil

COOK'S TIP

The mixture can also be used to make larger pancakes. Spread them with soured cream, sprinkle grated Cheddar cheese over, and roll them up neatly before serving hot.

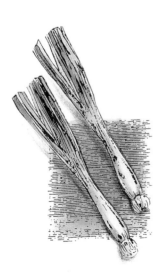

Put the shredded courgette in a bowl and add the chillies, garlic and chopped spring onions. Season with plenty of salt and pepper. Add the beaten egg and stir in lightly. Stir in the flour.

Heat the oil in a deep, heavy frying pan. Drop 1 tablespoon of the mixture into the pan and flatten it lightly with the back of a spoon. Add more mixture to make as many pancakes as the frying pan will hold comfortably.

Fry over medium heat for 2 to 3 minutes on each side, or until golden brown, turning over carefully so that the oil does not splatter. Drain on absorbent kitchen paper and keep hot. Before frying each new batch, stir the pancake mixture.

RANCH-STYLE EGGS

Serves 4

This started out as a breakfast dish in Mexico, but it is now served at any time, often with refried beans.

INGREDIENTS

4 tbsp corn oil

4 wheat or corn flour tortillas

3 shallots, finely chopped

I garlic clove, crushed

I or 2 red New Mexico chillies, seeded and chopped

150 g/6 oz peeled, seeded and chopped ripe tomatoes

I tbsp tomato purée mixed with 2 tbsp water

salt and pepper

4 eggs

4 tbsp refried beans (page 26)

sprigs of parsley, for the garnish

Heat I teaspoon of the oil in a fryin pan and fry a tortilla for 30 seconds on both sides until crisp. Drain and keep warm. Fry the remaining tortillas in the same way.

Heat 2 tablespoons of the remaining oil and sauté the shallots, garlic and chillies for 5 minutes. Stir in the tomatoes and tomato purée mixture and leave to simmer whilst you cook the eggs.

Heat the remaining oil and fry the eggs until cooked to your taste. Place a tortilla on a plate and top with an egg and some tomato sauce. Serve with refried beans and garnish with parsley.

SALADS AND VEGETABLES

GREEN MANGO SALAD

Serves 4

This salad is intentionally sour, but you can add more sugar if you like. The quantities do not need to be precise. Add the
ingredients in the proportions that suit you, to create the flavour balance you and your family will enjoy.

INGREDIENTS

30 g/1 oz unsweetened dessicated
coconut

200 g/8 oz green unripe mango flesh,
cut into long matchsticks

25 g/1 oz dried baby prawns

3 tbsp sliced shallots

5 fresh small green chillies, chopped

1 tbsp palm or soft dark brown sugar,
or to taste

fish sauce, to taste (optional)

lime juice, to taste (optional)

Dry-fry the dessicated coconut
in a frying pan until it is pale
brown in colour. Watch it carefully so
that it does not scorch.

Mix the coconut and mango
matchsticks in a bowl. Add the dried
prawns, sliced shallots, and chopped
chillies. Stir in the sugar. Mix well and
taste. If not salty enough add a little
fish sauce; if not sour enough, add
lime juice.

COOK'S TIP
If you cannot find unripe
mangoes, try this with peaches
or nectarines.

BEAN SPROUT SALAD

Serves 4 to 6

This is one of Korea's best loved salads. Crunchy and nutritious, it is often served with pre-dinner drinks in restaurants, so guests have something to nibble whilst waiting for their meal to arrive.

INGREDIENTS

675 g/1½ lb soya bean sprouts or mung bean sprouts

2 garlic cloves, minced

5 spring onions, with the white and green parts thinly sliced into rings

1 fresh hot red chilli, seeded and thinly sliced into rings

1 tbsp toasted sesame seeds

salt

Remove the roots from the bean sprouts, if necessary. Bring a saucepan of water to the boil, and add the bean sprouts. As soon as the water boils again, tip the bean sprouts into a colander and rinse under running cold water. Drain well, then squeeze out as much water as possible.

Tip the bean sprouts into a salad bowl and add the remaining ingredients. Serve at room temperature, or slightly chilled. It is not necessary to add a dressing.

CORN SALAD WITH ROASTED CHILLIES AND PEPPERS

Serves 6

This corn salad is spicy, but not too hot, and can be used as a relish with grilled meats. When possible, use corn cut from the cob, but frozen corn is acceptable. The salad is best when made several hours in advance so the flavours have a chance to blend, but not so long that it loses its crunch. If the salad is made ahead, the avocado should be cut and added just before serving.

INGREDIENTS

1 poblano chilli

1 sweet red pepper

300 g/3 oz fresh or frozen whole kernel corn

150 ml/¼ pint water

½ green pepper, seeded and diced

2 tomatoes, seeded and chopped

50 g/2 oz minced red onion

1 large avocado

DRESSING

60 ml/2.5 fl oz olive oil

3 tbsp lime juice

2 tbsp freshly chopped coriander

½ tsp ground cumin

1 garlic clove, minced

dash salt

dash pepper

Make the dressing by mixing the olive oil, lime juice, coriander, cumin, garlic, salt and pepper in a jar. Close the lid tightly and shake well. Set aside.

Roast the chilli and red pepper under the grill for about 10 minutes, turning often, until all sides are charred. Remove and place in a plastic bag, or in a bowl covered with several pieces of absorbent kitchen paper. Let steam for at least 10 minutes.

While the chilli and pepper are cooling, cook the corn. Put the water in a small pan, add the corn and bring to the boil. Cook for 5 minutes, then drain the corn and let it cool.

Remove the chilli and red pepper from the bag or bowl. Rub off the blackened skin, then remove the stems and seeds. Cut the chilli and pepper into narrow strips.

Place the chilli and pepper strips in a bowl, add the corn, then the green pepper, tomatoes and onion. Cut the avocado in half, remove the peel and seed and dice the flesh. Add to the salad. Pour over the dressing and toss lightly. Serve as soon as possible after adding the diced avocado.

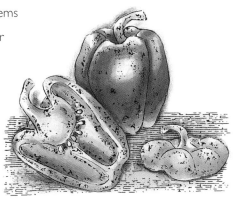

CUCUMBER SALAD WITH CHILLIES

Serves 4

It is important to observe the standing time when making this salad, so that all the flavours can blend.

INGREDIENTS

1 large cucumber, peeled

1 small red onion, thinly sliced

2 or 3 red serrano chillies, seeded and thinly sliced

2 tbsp lime juice

1 tbsp Thai fish sauce

2 tsp honey, warmed

1 tbsp sesame oil

rocket leaves

150 g/6 oz chopped roasted peanuts

Cut the cucumber in half lengthwise and cut into half-moon shapes. Place in a large shallow dish. Scatter the onion and chilli slices over the top.

Mix the lime juice, fish sauce and honey in a bowl. Whisk in the oil. Pour over the cucumber mixture, toss to coat, then leave in a cool place for at least 30 minutes to allow the flavours to develop.

Arrange the rocket leaves on a serving platter, top with the cucumber mixture and sprinkle with the roasted peanuts.

MIXED LEAVES WITH CHIPOTLE CHILLI DRESSING

Serves 4

Chipotle chillies give a delicious smoky flavour to the dressing. You can substitute any other dried chilli, if preferred, or use fresno chillies for a fresher flavour.

INGREDIENTS	DRESSING
150 g/4 oz rocket	6 dried chipotle chillies
a few small frisée and radicchio leaves	1 small onion, sliced
1 heart of lettuce	2 garlic cloves, minced
100 g/4 oz baby spinach leaves	3 tbsp medium-dry white wine
2 heads Belgian endive	3 tbsp white wine vinegar
1 small red onion, thinly sliced	2 tbsp tomato purée
3 tbsp assorted freshly chopped fresh herbs, such as coriander, flat-leaved parsley, oregano and marjoram	150 ml/¼ pint water

Make the dressing. Split the chillies and discard the seeds. Put into a pan with the remaining dressing ingredients. Cover the pan and cook over gentle heat for 45 minutes, or until the chillies are soft and the liquid is reduced by half.

Tip the contents of the pan into a blender or food processor. Process to a smooth purée, then press through a strainer set over a bowl. Reserve.

Lightly rinse all the salad leaves and the endive. Pat dry with absorbent kitchen paper. Tear the leaves if large, then toss together in a salad bowl.

Divide the endive into single leaves, and add to the salad with the onion and herbs. Mix together lightly. Just before serving, drizzle with the dressing, and toss to coat.

GREEN BEAN SALAD WITH PICKLED JALAPEÑOS

Serves 4 to 6

This is a variation on a famous Mexican salad based on *nopalitos,* which are young cactus shoots. If you have access to these – or can locate canned *nopalitos* – substitute them for the green beans.

INGREDIENTS

50 g/2 oz cut green beans

2 tomatoes, peeled, seeded and chopped

½ small onion, minced

2 or 3 drained pickled jalapeño chiles, seeded and sliced into strips

romaine leaves, to serve

crumbled fresh cheese, for the garnish

DRESSING

2 tbsp wine vinegar

1 tbsp freshly chopped coriander

large, pinch dried oregano

3 tbsp olive oil

salt and pepper

Make the dressing. Mix the vinegar, coriander and dried oregano in a small bowl. Whisk in the olive oil, then add salt and pepper to taste.

Combine the beans, tomatoes, onion and jalapeños in a bowl. Add the dressing and toss lightly.

Line a salad bowl with the romaine leaves. Spoon the dressed salad into the centre, and garnish with the crumbled fresh cheese.

COOK'S TIP
Use feta cheese for the garnish, if you like. It isn't remotely authentic, but tastes delicious with the beans and chillies.

POTATOES WITH CHILLI, PEANUTS AND CHEESE

Serves 4

Roast potatoes with a difference: adding onion, garlic and chillies creates a sensational dish, and the roasted peanuts on top are an inspirational extra.

INGREDIENTS

150 g/6 oz finely diced potatoes

1 large onion, sliced

2 garlic cloves, chopped

5 red fresno chillies

4 to 5 tbsp olive oil

salt and pepper

100 g/4 oz shelled raw peanuts

shavings of grated Parmesan cheese

Pre-heat the oven to 200°C/400°F/Gas Mark 6. Put the potatoes in a roasting pan and scatter the onion and garlic over.

Make a slit down each chilli and scrape out the seeds and membrane. Chop roughly. Sprinkle over the vegetables, drizzle with the oil, then add the seasoning. Turn the vegetables in the oil until evenly coated. Roast in the oven for 50 minutes, turning the vegetables occasionally. Scatter the peanuts over and continue to roast until golden. Transfer to a bowl and serve with shavings of Parmesan.

BRAISED OKRA WITH CHILLIES

Serves 4

Braising okra with onion, chillies, pepper and tomatoes really brings out the flavour of this unusual vegetable.

INGREDIENTS

450 g/1 lb okra

2 tbsp sunflower oil

1 large onion, thinly sliced

4 green Anaheim chillies, seeded and sliced

1 green pepper, seeded and sliced

150 g/6 oz peeled, seeded, and chopped tomatoes

salt and pepper

3 tbsp water

plain yoghurt, for serving

Trim the okra and prick each pod a few times with a fork.

Heat the oil in a pan and sauté the onion and chillies for 5 minutes, or until softened. Add the green pepper and cook for 2 minutes more.

Stir in the chopped tomatoes, okra and water, with seasoning to taste. Bring to the boil. Reduce the heat, cover the pan and simmer for 8 minutes, or until the okra is tender. Transfer to a bowl and serve immediately with spoonfuls of yoghurt.

▶ *(Above) Potatoes with Chilli, Peanuts and Cheese (Below) Braised Okra with Chillies*

RED RICE

Serves 4

INGREDIENTS

2 tbsp sunflower oil

I red onion, chopped

2 garlic cloves, chopped

5 red Anaheim chillies, seeded and chopped

6 sun-dried tomatoes, chopped

750–900 ml/16–28 fl oz vegetable stock

175 g/6 oz long-grain rice

I red pepper, seeded and chopped

2 tbsp tomato purée

salt and pepper

150 g/5 oz sweetcorn kernels

freshly chopped coriander, for the garnish

Pre-heat the oven to 180°C/ 350°F/Gas Mark 4. Heat the oil in a pan and gently sauté the onion, garlic, chillies and sun-dried tomatoes for 3 minutes. Add the stock and simmer for 10 minutes, or until the tomatoes are soft. Purée in a food processor, then transfer to a flame-proof casserole.

Add the rice and red pepper. Mix the tomato purée with 2 tablespoons of the remaining stock and stir into the tomato mixture. Add more of the stock and seasoning to taste.

Bring to the boil then cover and place in the oven. Cook for 30 minutes. Add the sweetcorn kernels with extra stock if necessary and cook for 10 minutes more, or until the rice is tender. Separate the grains with a fork and serve sprinkled with the coriander.

GREEN RICE

Serves 4

INGREDIENTS

2 tbsp sunflower oil

I large onion, chopped

2 garlic cloves, chopped

4 green Anaheim chillies, seeded and sliced

175 g/6 oz long-grain rice

I green pepper, seeded and chopped

600 ml/1 pint vegetable stock

salt and pepper

150 g/5 oz frozen peas

I tbsp freshly chopped parsley

2 tbsp pumpkin seeds, toasted

Heat the oil in a large, deep frying pan and sauté the onion, garlic and chillies for 3 minutes. Stir in the rice and green pepper, and sauté for 3 minutes more.

Pour in the stock and bring to the boil. Reduce the heat and simmer for 15 minutes, or until the rice is almost tender. Add a little more stock if necessary and stir occasionally during cooking.

Stir in the peas and seasoning to taste, and cook for 5 to 7 minutes more, or until the rice and peas are cooked. Adjust the seasoning and serve sprinkled with the parsley and toasted pumpkin seeds.

◄ *Above: Red Rice, Below: Green Rice*

FRAGRANT MUSHROOMS AND PEAS

Serves 4

Mushrooms yield quite a lot of liquid when sautéed. It is important to keep the heat under the pan fairly high so that this is driven off and the mixture is quite dry.

INGREDIENTS

300–375 g/12–15 oz button mushrooms

2 tbsp oil

1 small onion, finely sliced

¼ tsp cumin seeds, crushed

¼ tsp mustard seeds

2 tomatoes, chopped

1 fresh green chilli, minced

200 g/7 oz frozen peas

½ tsp chilli powder

¼ tsp turmeric

½ tsp salt

1 small red pepper, seeded and chopped

4 fat garlic cloves, minced

2 tbsp freshly chopped coriander

chopped spring onions or chives, for the garnish

Cut the small mushrooms into halves and the larger ones into quarters. Heat the oil in a pan and sauté the onion gently for 5 minutes. Add the cumin and mustard seeds and sauté for 2 to 3 minutes more.

Stir in the tomatoes and green chilli, followed by the mushrooms and peas. Stir-fry them for 2 to 3 minutes over medium heat.

Add the chilli powder, turmeric and salt, mixing well. Cook, uncovered for 5 to 7 minutes.

Finally, stir in the pepper, garlic and coriander and cook for 5 minutes more, until the mixture is quite dry. Garnish with the spring onions or chives.

AUBERGINE WITH POTATOES AND CHILLIES

Serves 4 to 6

INGREDIENTS

1 aubergine
2 potatoes
2 tbsp oil
½ onion, sliced
½ tsp cumin seeds
½ tsp roasted coriander seeds
3 to 4 curry leaves (optional)
1 tsp grated fresh root ginger
4 to 5 garlic cloves, finely chopped
½ tsp chilli powder
¼ tsp turmeric
salt to taste
200 ml/⅓ pint water
1 tbsp plain yoghurt
½ tsp sugar
1 to 2 fresh green chillies, chopped
1 green pepper, seeded and chopped
1 tomato, chopped
1 tbsp lemon juice
2 tbsp freshly chopped coriander

Cut the aubergine into quarters lengthwise, then, holding the pieces together, cut them across into 1.25 cm/½- inch chunks.

Scrub the potatoes thoroughly, but do not peel them. Cut each one into 12 bite-sized pieces.

Heat the oil in a heavy saucepan and sauté the onion for about 7 minutes until golden brown. Add the cumin and coriander seeds, with the curry leaves, if using. Fry for 1 to 2 minutes, then add the ginger, half the garlic, the chilli powder, turmeric and salt. Cook this mixture over a high heat for about 2 minutes, adding 2 tablespoons of the water if necessary so that the spice paste does not stick to the pan.

Add the aubergine then stir in the yoghurt, sugar and green chillies. Cook for 2 to 3 minutes. Add the remaining water, cover tightly, reduce the heat and simmer for 15 minutes.

Add the potato, pepper and tomato. Replace the lid and simmer for 10 minutes more. Check the mixture; add a little more water if needed. Lastly, add the remaining garlic, the lemon juice and the coriander. Cook for 1 minute more, gently stir to mix thoroughly, then serve.

SAUCES AND SALSAS

GREEN CHILLI SAUCE

Makes about 450 g/1 lb

Ideal to serve with egg dishes, chicken or as the basis of a stew or casserole.

INGREDIENTS

450 g/1 lb fresh green Anaheim chillies

1 large onion, quartered

3 garlic cloves, peeled

2 tbsp corn oil or olive oil

275 ml/½ pint chicken or vegetable stock

1 tsp salt

½ tsp black pepper

2 tbsp freshly chopped coriander

thinly sliced fresh chilli, for the garnish

Pre-heat the grill. Place the chillies, onion and garlic in the grill pan and drizzle with the oil. Grill for 5 to 8 minutes, or until the chillies have blistered and the skins blackened. Put the chillies into a plastic bag and leave to sweat for about 10 minutes, then rub off the skins.

Put the chillies with all the other ingredients into a food processor, except the coriander. Process to a chunky purée. Stir in the coriander and warm through just before serving. Garnish with the sliced chilli.

RED CHILLI PASTE

Makes about 340 g/12 oz

Use when extra heat is required in order to spice up soups, stews and casseroles.

INGREDIENTS

4 red habanero chillies, seeded

1 onion, chopped

2 garlic cloves, crushed

2 tsp ground coriander

1 tbsp freshly chopped coriander

2.5 cm piece of root ginger, peeled and grated

zest and juice of 2 limes

1 tsp salt

½ tsp black pepper

3 tbsp corn or olive oil

Rinse the chillies and put them in the top of a steamer over a pan of gently steaming water. Steam for 5 minutes or until soft. Alternatively, cover with hot water and leave for 15 minutes, then drain.

Put all the ingredients into a food processor and blend to a thick paste, adding a little extra oil if necessary. Transfer to a screw-top jar and store in the refrigerator. Use within 1 week.

▶ *(Clockwise from top left): Red Chilli Paste, Chilli Pepper Relish (p. 28), Green Chilli Sauce, Red Chilli Sauce*

RED CHILLI SAUCE

Makes about 340 g/12 oz

Both Green and Red Chilli-Sauce are used as a condiment for fish, meat and poultry or can be used as a dip.

INGREDIENTS

3 red serrano chillies

1 tbsp corn oil or olive oil

4 ripe tomatoes, peeled, seeded and chopped

4 shallots, finely chopped

2 garlic cloves, chopped

1 tsp ground cumin

1 tsp ground coriander

180 ml/6.5 fl oz vegetable or chicken stock

2 tbsp tomato purée

½ tsp salt

½ tsp black pepper

1 tbsp lime juice

2 tbsp freshly chopped coriander

Pre-heat the grill. Place the chillies in the grill pan and drizzle with the oil. Grill for 5 minutes, or until blackened and blistered. Put into a plastic bag and leave to sweat for 10 minutes, then rub off the skins and chop the flesh.

Put all the ingredients, except the coriander, into a food processor and blend to a thick purée. Pour into a frying pan and cook over gentle heat, stirring frequently, for 10 minutes.

CHILLI AND ANCHOVY SAUCE

Serves 4 to 6

This Thai sauce is not very spicy, but has an interesting combination of flavours.

INGREDIENTS

6 garlic cloves

1 tbsp sliced shallot

1 tsp chopped fresh root ginger

2 tbsp finely chopped anchovies

1 tbsp lemon juice

1 dried red chilli, pounded finely

1 kaffir-lime leaf, torn into small pieces

½ lemongrass stalk, with outer leaves removed and finely sliced

Dry-fry the garlic, shallot and ginger in a non-stick frying pan for 3 minutes, then chop finely. Pound with the rest of the ingredients using a mortar and pestle or a spice mill.

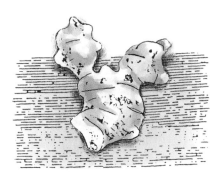

MEXICAN TOMATO SAUCE

Serves 4 to 6

Use this rich sauce with tortillas, over pasta, with grilled meat or even as a topping for steamed cauliflower.

INGREDIENTS

2 to 3 tbsp olive oil

2 large onions, finely chopped

3 or 4 garlic cloves, chopped

2 to 4 serrano chillies, chopped

700 g/24-oz tin tomatoes, chopped

175 g/6-oz tin tomato purée

200 ml/⅓ pint red wine

1 tbsp freshly chopped herbs (parsley, sage, rosemary, thyme, oregano)

salt and pepper

sugar to taste (optional)

2 tbsp freshly chopped coriander

Heat the oil in a pan. Add the onions and garlic and sauté for 5 to 8 minutes, until they are soft and golden. Add the chillies, tomatoes, tomato purée, wine, herbs and seasoning. Add sugar if the sauce is too sharp; this will depend on the wine and the tomatoes, and may not be necessary. Simmer for 15 to 30 minutes. Stir in the coriander before serving.

HOT, HOT, HOT PEPPER SAUCE

Makes about 450 g/1 lb

INGREDIENTS

225 ml/8 fl oz vinegar

7 tbsp lime or lemon juice

2 onions, minced

6 radishes, finely chopped

2 garlic cloves, minced

2 to 3 tbsp minced fresh hot chilli

4 tbsp olive oil

salt and pepper

Mix all the ingredients in a bowl, and serve. Store any leftover sauce in a tightly sealed glass jar.

SPICY MINCED BEEF SAUCE

Serves 4

Kenyan chillies could be used in this sauce if available, for a milder flavour. Use in tacos, enchiladas or burritos,

INGREDIENTS

1 tbsp corn or olive oil

1 onion, finely chopped

2 garlic cloves, crushed

2 Scotch Bonnet chillies, seeded and chopped

2 celery stalks, trimmed and finely chopped

350 g/12 oz minced beef

1 tbsp tomato purée mixed with 2 tbsp water

375 ml/13 fl oz peeled and chopped ripe tomatoes

1 tsp ground cilantro

1 tsp ground cumin

2 tbsp cider vinegar

1 tsp honey

2 tbsp freshly chopped oregano

Heat the oil in a frying pan and sauté the onion, garlic, chillies and celery for 5 minutes. Add the beef and cook, stirring frequently, for 5 to 8 minutes, or until browned.

Stir in the tomato purée mixture, with all the remaining ingredients. Bring to the boil, then reduce the heat and simmer for 45 minutes, or until the sauce is thick and flavourful.

AVOCADO SALSA

Makes about 550 g/20 oz

Avocado salsa is similar to guacamole, but the avocado is cubed rather than mashed, and is mixed with minced chillies. Use it as a dip for chips or a topping for chilli. You can mix the other ingredients in advance, but do not dice and add the avocados until just before serving. Remove the seeds and veins from the jalapeño chillies for a milder salsa.

INGREDIENTS

1 medium tomato, diced

½ medium red onion, finely chopped

2 fresh jalapeño chillies, minced

3 tbsp lime juice

1 tbsp olive oil

1 tbsp freshly chopped coriander

salt and pepper

3 avocados, diced

Combine the tomato, onion, chillies, lime juice, olive oil, and coriander in a bowl. Season to taste. Cover and set aside for several hours to allow the flavours to blend, if you have time. Cut the avocados in half and remove the peel and seeds. Dice all the flesh and gently stir it into the salsa just before serving.

PINEAPPLE SALSA

Serves 4

INGREDIENTS

200 ml/⅓ pint–225 ml/8 fl oz pineapple juice

1 garlic clove, chopped

1 green onion, thinly sliced

1 ripe tomato, finely chopped, or 50 g/2 oz tinned tomato juice or crushed tomatoes

1 tbsp freshly chopped mint

1 tbsp freshly chopped coriander

hot pepper sauce, to taste

dash each of ground cumin and sugar

juice of ½ lime plus a little of the zest

salt

Mix all the ingredients in a bowl, cover and let rest for 30 minutes to allow the flavours to develop.

▶ *Avocado Salsa*

PICKLES AND CHUTNEYS

GARLIC AND CHILLI EXTRACT

A few drops of this extract really perks up soups and stews, but because the flavour is very intense, it should be used with caution. The quantities of garlic and chillies listed are merely a guide and may vary depending on the size of the bottle selected, and on personal taste.

INGREDIENTS

10 garlic cloves

5 small fresh green chillies

cooking sherry

Peel the garlic cloves and cut them in half. Prick the chillies all over. Mix them together and pack into a clean, dry wine bottle.

Cover with the sherry and fill the bottle, leaving room for the cork. Cork the bottle securely and leave, undisturbed, in a cool, dark place for a couple of weeks.

The sherry can be topped up from time to time.

COOK'S TIP

A bottle of this extract makes a great gift for a keen cook. Use pale sherry for the best effect, and label the bottle with a warning that the contents should be used with care.

INDONESIAN HOT VEGETABLE PICKLE

Serves 4

Peanuts and pineapple are pepped up with chilli in this spicy pickle. It is often served with curries, cold meat or even fish dishes.

INGREDIENTS

4 fresh red Thai chillies

1 large onion, chopped

3 garlic cloves

200 g/8 oz fresh roasted peanuts

3 tbsp sunflower oil

3 tbsp sugar

600 ml/1 pint white wine vinegar

150 g/6 oz cut green beans

1 cucumber, peeled and diced

2 red peppers, seeded and chopped

150 g/6 oz small cauliflower florets

1 fresh pineapple, with flesh removed from shell, cored and diced

salt and pepper

a few threads of saffron or ½ tsp turmeric

Put the chillies, onion and garlic into a food processor and process until smooth. Reserve. Grind or process the peanuts until lightly chopped and reserve.

Heat the oil in a large pan and gently cook the chilli purée for 4 minutes. Add the sugar and vinegar, bring to the boil, then lower the heat and simmer for 5 minutes.

Add the peanut paste and then the vegetables and pineapple with the seasoning and saffron or turmeric. Simmer for 2 minutes, stirring constantly. If serving hot, heat through gently for 4 to 5 minutes, stirring frequently. If serving cold, heat through for 2 minutes, then place in a serving dish, cover and chill. Stir thoroughly before serving.

If stored in sealed screw-top glass jars, the pickle can be kept in the refrigerator or a cool place for up to 1 month.

▶ *Garlic and Chilli Extract*

CORN AND CHILLI RELISH

Makes about 900 g/2 lb

The sweetcorn kernels used to make this light, unthickened relish should either be freshly cut or frozen; tinned sweetcorn would not hold their shape. You can either use the relish immediately or you can bottle it for use within two months.

INGREDIENTS

2 fresh green or red chillies

1 green pepper

100 g/4 oz sweetcorn kernels

2 tbsp sugar

½ tsp salt

¼ tsp mustard powder

450 ml/¾ pint white wine vinegar

Remove the seeds from the chillies and finely chop them. Core, seed and finely chop the pepper. Put the chillies and peppers into a saucepan and add the sweetcorn.

In a bowl, mix together the sugar, salt and mustard powder. Gradually stir in the vinegar, then pour the mixture into the pan. Bring to the boil, then lower the heat and simmer for 15 minutes, or until the sweetcorn is just tender.

Let the relish cool completely. Serve immediately or store in a covered container in the refrigerator for use within one week. Alternatively, spoon it, whilst still warm, into warm, sterilised jars and seal immediately. Once opened, use within 1 week.

CARIBBEAN MANGO CHUTNEY

Makes about 2.25 kg/5 lb

Very dark in colour, this is a rich, hot and fruity chutney that still retains the fresh mango taste. Leave it for two weeks before opening. Once opened, it will keep for up to one month. Unopened, it will keep for up to two years.

INGREDIENTS

6 under-ripe mangoes

1 tbsp salt

50 g/2 oz dried tamarind

6 tbsp boiling water

225 g/8 oz raisins, soaked for 12 hours

3 cups malt vinegar

50 g/2 oz fresh root ginger, peeled and grated

2 fresh red or green chillies, seeded and finely chopped

2 garlic cloves, minced

400 g/14 oz soft dark brown sugar

Peel and dice the mangoes. Put them into a bowl, stir in the salt and leave them for 2 hours. Do not drain them. Put the tamarind into a bowl, pour the boiling water over it and leave for 30 minutes. Drain the tamarind, sieving the pulp into a bowl.

Put the raisins into a preserving pan or saucepan. Add the vinegar, mangoes, tamarind pulp, ginger, chillies, garlic and sugar. Bring to the boil, lower the heat and simmer for about 1 hour, or until the mixture is thick. The mangoes should be tender but still in recognizable pieces.

Spoon the hot chutney into warm, sterilized jars and seal immediately.

PICKLED PEARS WITH CHILLIES

Makes about 900 g/2 lb

Tender, mildly spiced slices of pear in a sharp-sweet pickle sauce are an excellent way to make use of cheap and plentiful fruit in the fall. Keep the pickle for one week before using. Unopened, it will keep for up to six months. Once opened, it must be eaten within one week.

INGREDIENTS

1 cinnamon stick, broken

6 cloves

2.5 cm/1 inch piece of fresh root ginger, bruised

600 ml/1 pint white wine vinegar

675 g/1½ lb sugar

6 small pears (about 2 kg/4 lb)

dried red chillies, one for each jar

Tie the cinnamon, cloves and root ginger in a small piece of muslin. Put the spice bag into a saucepan with the vinegar and sugar. Set the pan over low heat and stir until the sugar has dissolved. Bring the syrup to the boil and remove the pan from the heat.

Bring a saucepan of water to the boil. Meanwhile, peel and quarter the pears and cut out their cores. Cook the pears in the boiling water for 5 minutes, then drain them.

Bring the syrup to the boil again and add the pears. Reduce the heat, and simmer the pears for about 15 minutes, until they are tender but still firm and they look translucent.

Using a slotted spoon, lift the pears out of the syrup and pack them into warm, sterilized jars. Put one dried chilli into each jar.

Lift out the spice bag from the syrup and boil the syrup again for about 5 minutes. Pour the hot syrup over the pears. Seal immediately.

TOMATO AND GREEN PEPPER RELISH

Makes about 1.25 kg/2½ lb

Good with burgers, sausages and all barbecue food, this rich tomato relish can be served immediately or it can be kept in a covered container in the refrigerator for up to two weeks.

INGREDIENTS

8 tomatoes

4 tbsp olive oil

1 onion, finely chopped

1 garlic clove, minced

1 green pepper, cored, seeded, and diced

1 or 2 small fresh green chillies, seeded and diced (optional)

2 tbsp soft dark brown sugar

4 tbsp malt vinegar

Put the tomatoes into a large heat-proof bowl. Pour boiling water over them and leave for 1 minute, then drain, skin, and chop them.

Heat the oil in a saucepan over low heat. Cook the onion and garlic for 2 minutes, then stir in the peppers and chillies and cook for 2 minutes more, stirring occasionally, until they begin to soften.

Increase the heat to medium and add the tomatoes. Stir until heated through, then stir in the sugar. When it has melted, add the vinegar and bring it to the boil. Remove the pan from the heat and let the relish cool completely.

► *Pickled Pears with Chillies*

PICCALILLI

Makes about 2.75 kg/6 lb

Almost any combination of crunchy vegetables can be used to make this mustard pickle, but the selection below works very well. Leave the pickle for one week before using. Unopened, it will keep for up to three months. Once opened, it should be eaten within two weeks.

INGREDIENTS

1 large cucumber
6 courgettes (about 50 g/1 lb)
1 large cauliflower (about 1 kg/2 lb)
4 onions
2 tbsp salt
900 ml/1½ pt distilled malt vinegar
1 tbsp mustard seeds
1 tsp black peppercorns
4 dried red chillies
150 g/4 oz soft brown sugar
2 tsp ground ginger
1 tbsp ground turmeric
1 tbsp mustard powder
2 tsp flour

Wipe but do not peel the cucumber; cut it into 1 cm/¼ inch dice. Wipe the courgettes and thinly slice them. Divide the cauliflower into small florets. Chop the onions.

Put all the chopped vegetables into a large bowl and add the salt. Toss well. Leave for 12 hours. Drain the vegetables in a colander, rinse them through with cold water, and then drain them again.

Pour 600 ml/1 pint of the vinegar into a saucepan and add the mustard seeds, peppercorns and chillies. Bring to the boil, reduce the heat, cover and simmer for 10 minutes. Strain the vinegar and return it to the saucepan. Stir in the sugar until dissolved.

Put the ginger, turmeric, mustard powder and flour into a small bowl and gradually mix in the remaining vinegar. Stir the mixture into the hot vinegar in the saucepan. Bring the mixture to the boil and stir in the vegetables. Reduce the heat and simmer for 10 minutes, stirring occasionally.

Let the pickle cool completely then pack it into cold, sterilized jars. Seal the jars immediately.

SWEET SPICED ONION SLICES

Makes about 2.25 kg/5 lb

Dried chillies and cloves flavour this sweet onion pickle. Small button mushrooms can be pickled in the same way: peel them and salt them whole, then proceed with the recipe as for sliced onions. Leave the pickle for one week before using. Unopened, it will keep for up to four months but once opened, it should be eaten within one week.

INGREDIENTS

12 onions (about 1.5 kg/3 lb)
2 tbsp salt
600 ml/1 pint white wine vinegar
225 g/8 oz sugar
1 tbsp cloves
12 dried red chillies

Slice the onions very thinly into rings. Layer them in a bowl with the salt, cover and leave for 12 hours. Rinse the onions with cold water and drain them well.

Put the vinegar, sugar, cloves and chillies into a saucepan and stir them over a low heat until the sugar has melted. Bring to the boil, reduce the heat and simmer gently for 5 minutes.

Pack the onions into warm, sterilized jars. Pour the hot vinegar over them, ensuring the cloves and chillies are evenly distributed among the jars. Seal immediately.

GARLIC AND CHILLI JELLY

This is a very good relish with roasts and cold cuts. Its clear colour and excellent flavour make it a good candidate for a food stand at a fair.

INGREDIENTS

175 g/4 lb sour apples

2 heads garlic (about 25 cloves)

10 small fresh red chillies

1.2 litres/2 pints water

sugar (see method)

Cut the apples into 2.5 cm/1 inch chunks, but do not peel or core them. Separate and peel the garlic cloves and cut each in half lengthwise. Cut the chillies in half.

Put the apples, garlic and chillies into a kettle pan with the water and stew for about 1 hour, until the apples are reduced to pulp. Tip into a jam bag or thick cloth, and leave to drain overnight. Do not be tempted to speed up the flow of juice by squeezing the bag, as this will only make the juice cloudy.

Measure the juice into a clean pan and add 450 g/1 pound of sugar for every 600 ml/2 pints of liquid. Stir over gentle heat until the sugar has dissolved. Boil rapidly for 10 minutes, until a little of the jelly sets when cooled on a plate, and wrinkles when you push it with your finger.

While the jelly is still hot, pour it into dry, warmed jars, filling them almost to the brim. Cover the surface of the jelly with a disk of waxed paper. Put a cellophane or waxed paper cover over each jar, secure with thin twine or an elastic band and store in a dark, cool, dry place.

INDEX